ANOREXIA

ANOREXIA

Other Books in the At Issue Series:

ANOREXIA

Daniel A. Leone, *Book Editor*

David L. Bender, *Publisher*
Bruno Leone, *Executive Editor*

Bonnie Szumski, *Editorial Director*
Stuart B. Miller, *Managing Editor*

An Opposing Viewpoints® Series

Greenhaven Press, Inc.
San Diego, California

Library of Congress Cataloging-in-Publication Data

Anorexia / Daniel A. Leone, book editor.
        p.   cm. — (At issue)
    Includes bibliographical references and index.
    ISBN 0-7377-0467-5 (pbk.: alk. paper) —
ISBN 0-7377-0468-3 (lib.: alk. paper)
    1. Anorexia nervosa. 2. Anorexia nervosa—Social aspects.
I. Leone, Daniel A., 1969–   . II. At issue (San Diego, Calif.)

RC552.A5 .A547 2001
616.85'262—dc21   00-047698
                                                                          CIP

©2001 by Greenhaven Press, Inc., PO Box 289009,
San Diego, CA 92198-9009

Printed in the U.S.A.

Table of Contents

Introduction

Kelly, a sixteen-year-old high school student, was slowly dying. At five feet, three inches, she was of normal height, but her body weight had dropped from a healthy and normal 125 pounds to a dangerous reading of barely 50 pounds. Her weight loss began at fourteen when she pleaded with her mother to allow her to go on a partial liquid diet so she could lose a few pounds. Her mother, thinking this was just a harmless phase her daughter was going through, reluctantly approved. Within a few months Kelly lost 25 pounds and was hospitalized by her mother when she nearly passed out on a walk they had taken together. She was treated for a few days and then released since her condition was not life-threatening. However, Kelly did not admit or recognize that she had a serious problem. Over the next couple years, her obsession with weight worsened as she dropped down to as low as 50 pounds, 40 percent of her normal body weight. Seeing that Kelly was weak, listless, and skeletal, her mother once again checked her into a hospital. After a four-month struggle, Kelly finally acknowledged her eating disorder and began a recovery. When she was released from the hospital, she weighed 102 pounds and eventually reached a more normal weight of 115 pounds. Although Kelly still struggles to resist her urges to lose weight, she is happy to be alive.

Kelly suffers from an eating disorder called anorexia nervosa, more commonly known as anorexia. She is not alone. It is estimated that between 6 and 10 million women and another million young men suffer from an eating disorder of some kind, most frequently either anorexia or bulimia. Bulimia, which is characterized by binge eating and purging, is the more common eating disorder. But an estimated one percent of all teenage girls suffer from anorexia, which is characterized by an obsession with dieting and weight loss.

The *American Anorexia Bulimia Association* defines anorexia as a disorder in which preoccupation with dieting and thinness leads to excessive weight loss. Along with this preoccupation, anorexics develop a distorted body image and think they are fat even though they are dangerously thin. A person is considered to have anorexia when his or her dieting reduces the body's weight to 85 percent of what would be considered normal.

Anorexia, although not as prevalent as bulimia, is generally considered to be the more serious and deadly disorder. According to researchers, more than 10 percent of all cases end in death. Anorexia is also more difficult to treat successfully than bulimia. A recent study conducted by Harvard Medical School of 245 women undergoing treatment for eating disorders found that while 74 percent of bulimics had a full recovery, only 33 percent of anorexics fully recovered from their disease. With such a low recovery rate it is easy to understand why anorexia is such a cause for concern.

The causes of anorexia

What could cause a person to intentionally starve herself to the point of death? Many experts believe that anorexic behavior is usually triggered by external influences and factors. One widely held belief is that the media and society's emphasis on body size and thinness encourages anorexic behavior in vulnerable teens and children. In her popular book, *Afraid to Eat*, nutritionist Frances Berg contends, "It's irrational, but kids are succumbing to the same destructive cultural messages about body and weight that plague adults. Instead of growing up with secure and healthy attitudes about their bodies, eating and themselves, many kids fear food and fear being fat." Other experts suggest that dysfunctional parents and family life contribute directly to anorexia. They argue that demanding parents can send a message to a child that nothing they do is good enough, causing them to work harder and harder for approval. In a culture that places such a high value on thinness, losing weight can easily be seen as a way of gaining that approval. Sometimes, too, when a family is under stress, such as a divorce, a child may use eating habits as a way to regain some sense of control in her life.

Other eating disorder specialists contend that anorexic behavior comes from internal sources but is triggered by outside influences. They argue that some children are predisposed to anorexia in that they have a poor self-image or are ultra-sensitive. When they are subjected to stresses such as a divorce or excessive peer pressure, they lack the inner resources to handle such matters and may express their unhappiness through their eating habits.

Some experts see anorexia as having a distinct cause. Peggy Claude-Pierre, the director and founder of the Montreux Clinic for eating disorder patients, contends that some children are born with what she calls Confirmed Negativity Condition (CNC). Children with CNC view the world differently than others do. According to Claude-Pierre, these children feel a heightened sense of responsibility at an early age to solve the problems of their families, society, and the world. When they inevitably fail, they feel worthless and become withdrawn and detached. She contends that this negative view of oneself triggers anorexic behavior and that to cure an anorexic one must first reverse the CNC. As she states in her book, *The Secret Language of Eating Disorders*, "I have come to believe that CNC precedes the eating disorder and is at the root of these devastating illnesses. The eating disorder is the symptom; CNC is the affliction we must cure."

Anorexia is a complex, formidable, and growing problem that continues to plague teenagers and many adults as well. Baffling researchers and healthcare providers alike, anorexia promises to trouble humankind for the foreseeable future. *At Issue: Anorexia* explores this horrible and enigmatic disease through personal narratives of anorexics as well as professional opinions of eating disorder specialists and researchers.

1

Anorexia Nervosa: An Overview

Wellness Web

Wellness Web is a website created through the collaboration of pa-tients, healthcare professionals, and caregivers. Their mission is to help individuals find the best and most appropriate health information available.

Anorexia nervosa is an eating disorder that generally affects women from ages fifteen to thirty-five. It is defined as self-starva-tion to the point of reducing body weight to the level of 15 per-cent below normal. In its early stages, the disease often goes unde-tected because it is masked as a standard diet. There are a number of factors believed to contribute to the onset of anorexia, includ-ing extreme dieting, societal pressure to be thin, and family prob-lems. However, most experts believe that ultimately anorexics are driven by a need for control in their lives. Intervention and ther-apy are critical for anorexics since the disease is life-threatening. Unfortunately, many anorexics resist treatment and remain in a state of denial about their condition.

A norexia nervosa is an eating disorder that usually strikes women. Of the seven million women aged fifteen to thirty-five who have an eat-ing disorder, many will die from the complications of anorexia.

Probably the most famous case is that of Karen Carpenter, who died from heart failure resulting from anorexia nervosa. This disease can be de-fined as self-starvation leading to a loss of body weight 15 percent below normal, accompanied with hyperactivity, hypothermia, and amenorrhea. Hypothermia results when the body's natural insulation (fat stores) be-come nonexistent and the victim becomes cold all the time. Amenorrhea is the absence of at least three menstrual cycles—this is also affected by the loss of fat stores in the body.

Anorexia may not be noticed in the early stages because it often starts as an innocent diet. Anorexics often become hyperactive because they ex-ercise frantically in an attempt to burn calories to lose weight.

Reprinted from "Anorexia Nervosa," from Wellweb.com. Reprinted with permission from the Center for Current Research.

In the later and more dangerous stages, the disease may not be noticed by family members because the anorexic usually wears layered and baggy clothes.

Even though the anorexic is emaciated, she still feels "fat" and wants to hide her "ugly, fat body." An anorexic may have ritualistic eating patterns such as cutting her food into tiny pieces and weighing every piece of food before she eats it. These behaviors can be found in people who are on a normal, healthy diet, but in anorexics these behaviors are extremely exaggerated.

A number of research projects involving experimental preventive measures have been reported in the current medical literature. Some of these experiments may prove to be helpful either in reducing the risk of anorexia nervosa, or perhaps preventing it altogether:

(1) instruction on the harmful effects of unhealthy weight regulation;

(2) intervention with programs of weight regulation by practicing sound nutrition and dietary principles and beginning a regimen of aerobic physical activity; and

(3) development of coping skills for resisting the diverse sociocultural influences that appear linked to the current popular obsessions with thinness and dieting.

Current research

There are many reasons as to why women develop anorexia nervosa. One is that it is dieting taken to a dangerous extreme.

Another is that societal pressures dictate a woman be thin in order to be beautiful—the "waif look" was recently popular. But what these theories come down to is an issue of control. Whatever else is going on in the anorexic's life, the one thing that she feels she can control is food.

When problems in the family contribute to the feeling of loss of control, family therapy has provided a 90 percent improvement rate (Nichols and Schwartz, 1991). Behavior therapy is also used to change the eating patterns of an anorexic who is seriously close to death. This is usually after the anorexic has been tube-fed to prevent death.

Group and individual therapy has also proved effective—it depends on the person and the situation. But it is usually very difficult for these interventions to be implemented because the anorexic is almost always in denial. She cannot recognize that there is a problem because she still feels and sees herself as being fat.

Anorexia may not be noticed in the early stages because it often starts as an innocent diet.

If you know of someone who needs to be approached about an eating disorder, be prepared for resistance. Approach her when you think there is little chance of being interrupted. Know what you want to say, stay calm, and do not let the conversation escalate.

Offer caring support, and supply information about sources where anorexics can obtain help in your community (Graves, 1994). Do these things, and anything else necessary to facilitate intervention, because she is slowly killing herself.

Intervention is especially important, since recent research indicates that women suffering from anorexia nervosa are at much greater risk of dying than either female psychiatric patients, or the general population at large (Sullivan, 1995).

Another study involving a ten-year follow-up of 76 severely anorexic women has also shown such patients require intensive, on-going intervention to help them maintain normal weight and to help them avoid unsuitable eating behavior (Eckert and others, 1995).

Although as yet highly speculative, a recent study has indicated the possibility that viral infections may play a causative role in some cases of anorexia nervosa (Park, Lawrie, and Freeman, 1995).

Another new study indicates the possibility that children who display anxiety disorders between the ages of five and fifteen may be expressing the first indication of a biological vulnerability for anorexia nervosa. (Deep and others, 1995).

Generally speaking, early detection and treatment of this disease holds the greatest likelihood for positive outcomes (review: Woodside, 1995).

Bodily effects

In a recent paper (Leibowitz, 1992) the neurochemical-neuroendocrine systems in the brain controlling macronutrient intake and metabolism are discussed. According to the author,

> appetite, energy balance, and body weight-gain are modulated by diverse neurochemical and neuroendocrine signals from different organs in the body and diverse regions in the brain.
>
> The hypothalamus plays an important integrative function in this process, acting through a variety of systems that involve a close interaction between nutrients, amines, neuropeptides, and hormones.
>
> These systems underlie normal nutrient intake and metabolism and are thought to be responsible for shifts in feeding behavior across the circadian cycle and fluctuations relating to gender and age in both rats and humans.
>
> Moreover, alterations in these normal neurochemical-neuroendocrine systems may be associated with abnormal eating patterns, such as anorexia nervosa, bulimia, and obesity.
>
> Understanding the systems that control eating behavior might provide a foundation for the treatment and possible prevention of such disorders.

In another study (Patton, 1992) dieting itself was examined relative to its role in anorexia nervosa. According to the author, dieting in young women is for the most part a transient and benign activity without longer-term consequences.

However, a group of dieters do progress to develop the symptoms and behavior of eating disorders, so that dieting has been associated with an eight-fold rise in the risk of later eating disorder.

Dieting or factors closely associated may account for most eating disorders in young women. Many antecedents of eating disorder appear to operate through increasing the risk of dieting rather than determining eating disorders specifically. Only the development of further neurotic and depressive symptoms characterizes dieters progressing to eating disorders.

As the evidence implicating dieting in the origin of eating disorders becomes stronger so strategies for primary prevention become clearer.

Notes

American Psychiatric Association, 1987. Quick Reference to the Diagnostic Criteria form DSM-III-R (Washington, DC: APA, 1987), pages 63–64.

Deep and others, 1995. Premorbid onset of psychopathology in long-term recovered anorexia nervosa. International Journal of Eating Disorders (April 1995), volume 17(3), pages 291–297.

Eckert and others, 1995. Ten-year follow-up of anorexia nervosa. Psychological Medicine (January 1995), volume 25(1), pages 143–156.

Graves, 1994. How to help a friend with an eating disorder. Self (April 1994), pages 76–78.

Killen, Taylor, Hammer, Litt, Wilson, Rich, Hayward, Simmonds, Kraemer, and Varady, 1993. An attempt to modify unhealthful eating attitudes and weight regulation practices of young adolescent girls. International Journal of Eating Disorders (May 1993), volume 13(4), pages 369–384.

Leibowitz, 1992. Neurochemical-neuroendocrine systems in the brain controlling macronutrient intake and metabolism. Trends in Neurosciences (December 1992), volume 15(12), pages 491–497.

Nichols and Schwartz, 1991. Family Therapy: Concepts and Methods. 2nd Edition. M.P. Nichols and R.C. Schwartz, editors (Boston: Allyn & Bacon, 1991), page 477.

Park, Lawrie, and Freeman, 1995. Post-viral onset of anorexia nervosa. British Journal of Psychiatry (March 1995), volume 166(3), pages 386–389.

Patton, 1992. Eating disorders: antecedents, evolution and course. Annals of Medicine (August 1992), volume 24(4), pages 281–285.

Sullivan, 1995. Mortality in anorexia nervosa. American Journal of Psychiatry (July 1995), volume 152(7), pages 1073–1074.

Woodside, 1995. A review of anorexia nervosa and bulimia nervosa. Current Problems in Pediatrics (February 1995), volume 25(2), pages 67–89.

2

The Signs of Anorexia

Felicia Romeo

Felicia Romeo is a contributor to Education *magazine.*

Because anorexics often go to great lengths to hide their bodies and behavior and are usually in a state of denial, anorexia is often a difficult disease to detect. However, it is important to look for the early signs and symptoms of anorexia nervosa. These include refusing to maintain a normal body weight, intense fear of gaining weight, holding an exaggerated perception of body size, excessive exercise, and, in women, loss of menstrual cycle. The earlier anorexic behavior is identified the more likely that intervention and treatment can be successful.

Anorexia nervosa is a serious mental disorder, with onset occurring during adolescent years, which predominantly affects women in approximately 90 percent of the cases. The young girl who is psychologically vulnerable may be victim to this life-threatening disorder. The long-term mortality from anorexia nervosa is over 10 percent. These girls are among the student population in our nation's elementary and secondary schools. It is important that educators be familiar with the early stages of this disorder. However, more importantly, the educator must look for signs that indicate whether this student is just a typical dieter or a potential anorectic. Early identification increases the chances of a more favorable prognosis.

The purpose of this paper is to present a case description of a young girl who is in the early stages of anorexia nervosa. The inception of this disorder is very subtle, as it resembles the dieting behaviors of the typical adolescent who engages in the pursuit of a reasonable expectation of weight loss. This case description intends to inform the educator about the symptoms of anorexia nervosa, as it blends into what appears to be a normal diet. The major symptoms of anorexia nervosa include the following:

Some girls with anorexia nervosa display some of the following symptoms described in the Diagnostic and Statistics Manual IV:

• Refusal to maintain body weight at or above a minimally normal weight for age and height (body weight less than 85 percent of that expected).

Reprinted from Felicia Romeo, "Educators and the Onset of Anorexia Nervosa in Young Girls," *Education*, September 1, 1996. Reprinted with permission from Project Innovation.

• Intense fear of gaining weight or becoming fat, even though underweight.

• Exhibits a significant disturbance in the perception of the shape or size of his or her body, or denial of seriousness of the current low body weight.

• Postmenarcheal females with this disorder are amenorrhea (absence of at least three consecutive menstrual cycles).

• Usually weight loss is accomplished primarily through reduction in total food intake.

• Increased or excessive exercise.

The following case description is written in an informal format. The purpose of this presentation is to provide a realistic description and to challenge the reader to look for the signs of anorexia nervosa within the common ordinary experience of observing and relating to these young student girls on a daily basis in our nation's schools.

The initial stages of anorexia nervosa

A young girl wakes up one morning eager to begin her day. What will she wear? She looks among the varied colors of clothes in her closet and chooses a blue skirt, a skirt which she has not worn for some time. Her choice gives her a feeling of success as she continues her morning preparations for school. When she puts on the blue skirt, she notices it fits a little snugly and that she is having difficulty buttoning it at the waist. Has she gained weight? Didn't one of her friends recently comment that she looked "chubby"? She moves quickly toward the bathroom and steps on the scale. Sure enough. That is it. Yes, she weighs four pounds more than she did a few days ago when she weighed herself. There is only one solution: she will have to go on a diet. Certainly she is not going to let herself weigh as much as another girl in school who everyone knows is as fat as a balloon!

Our young dieter joins the family for breakfast and announces that she is going on a diet. This announcement is greeted by her family with benevolent amusement. A diet! She has decided that she will not eat any more junk food like potato chips and candy. Everyone in the family agrees that junk foods are not beneficial for you. Although she is not really overweight, they applaud her idea and agree with her initial plan.

The long-term mortality from anorexia nervosa is over 10 percent.

She intends to lose just a few pounds. She will eat a little less than her usual amount. As she drinks her breakfast juice, she begins to silently ask herself a few questions: How many calories are there in orange juice, toast and eggs? What foods should she eat? How much should she eat? She makes a mental note to herself that later in the day she will go to the school library and look up information concerning nutrition and dieting. She exits from the breakfast table with fantastic speed and without eating her toast.

During school she tells her friends that she has started a diet because she wants to lose six pounds. At lunch, the girls talk about the successes and failures of their own dieting attempts. They gleefully gossip about the shapes of other classmates who, of course, are not seated at the table. "Have you seen Jeanie's thighs? Wow, they are huge. She definitely wins the Ms. Thunderthighs of the Year award." The conversation continues along this topic for some time. A roster of girls' names is brought up and each girl's figure is critically evaluated for its weaknesses.

The conversation suddenly switches to just as careful an inspection of the food which they are eating for lunch. "Do you know how many calories there are in that little cookie? Probably a million. Well, not really, but hundreds for sure. I would not touch that cookie. You might gain weight by just touching it with your fingers."

Our teenage dieter leaves that lunch table and goes directly to the school library. She checks out a few nutrition books. During her history class, she has difficulty resisting the temptation to read the books. After this class, she will have science. She considers showing her science teacher the library books and asking the teacher's opinion. Our teenage dieter asks the science teacher for some advice about dieting. Also, she stops by a bookstore on the way home to buy the current best-selling diet book.

A diet plan

As a result of reading the diet and nutrition books, our teenage dieter decides to make a diet plan. In general, she is going to decrease the number of calories she consumes, by one-half, and decrease the portion size of each meal, by half. Certain foods will be on her forbidden list, such as fatty foods and carbohydrates. They contain too many calories. Foods which will be considered "safe" must be labeled "dietetic."

This morning when our teenage dieter steps on the scale, she notices she has lost two pounds. She greets this news with mixed emotions. On the one hand, she is glad that she lost some weight, but on the other hand, she wishes that it was more at this point in her diet. Our young dieter was jogging about a mile every day. Now she decides that she will increase her mile to three miles a day. This way she will "burn off" more calories. Exercise was definitely recommended and encouraged in every book that she had read concerning dieting. She will try to add another mile at the end of the week. She will never let anything interfere with her exercise schedule.

As she looks at the clock, she notices that it is still early and that most of her family is still in bed. Last night she woke up around one o'clock but managed to go back to sleep. Now it is only six o'clock. Our teenage dieter decides to do some sit-ups, jumping jacks and toe touches before she goes to breakfast. After all, she should take advantage of the available time. She knows that there is nothing to lose by exercising, but there is everything to gain. She quickly corrects herself and concludes there is more to gain if she does not exercise! With this thought, she softly accompanies each motion of her exercise with the rhythmical count: one, two, three, four, one, two . . . and so on.

The young dieter almost finishes sixty sit-ups when she hears her mother call her for breakfast. She would love to skip breakfast. Plus, she is full of so much energy she believes that she could probably do at least a hundred more of these exercises. Reluctantly, she goes down the stairs and gloomily looks at the breakfast meal. She eats half of everything on her plate and runs off to school. She has now lost more than twelve pounds and still fears that she is too fat. Her parents urge her to finish her breakfast and tell her that she is too thin. Our young dieter staunchly declares that she is still too fat and that she must lose more weight.

She will never let anything interfere with her exercise schedule.

The young dieter has been on her diet for a few months and she has been successfully losing weight. Her school friends comment that she does everything else so successfully, i.e., school work, plays in the band, etc., that they are not surprised at her achievement. While the lunch conversation is still very much occupied with dieting and body shapes, one girl comments that throughout the morning she has been having terrible menstrual cramps. The other girls join in a chorus about the horrors associated with their menstruation. This conversation brings to the attention of our teenage dieter for the first time that she has not menstruated in a few months. The young dieter reluctantly states to her friends that she has missed some menstrual periods, however she is not concerned.

Parents and adolescent peers

Initially, the young dieter receives considerable praise from her friends and parents regarding her weight loss. They notice it. They notice her. Many people comment about the "slenderness" of her appearance and how "fashionable" she looks. Our teenage dieter begins to feel that others admire her resolve and envy her. After all, glamorous models in fashion magazines, TV actresses and movie stars are all attractive and thin. She asks herself quietly, should she stop her dieting now, or should she continue until she loses just a few more pounds? She actively resists any suggestion from her peers or parents that she is too thin and must gain weight. Our young dieter believes that others are just jealous and is firmly convinced that she still looks too fat! Although she has lost more than 20 percent of her original weight (which was normal by the Metropolitan Life Insurance Charts), she is still afraid to eat more for fear that she will be fat!

This is a case description of a young girl in the early stages of anorexia nervosa and progressing further into the disorder. The educator can inquire, gently, with the young girl about her dieting behavior and listen for clues associated with the disorder. More importantly, the educator can also inquire of the young girl's friends to learn about the young dieter's behavior outside the classroom. In a parent conference the educator is able to learn about the young dieter's behavior at home.

Educators who are informed of the symptoms of anorexia nervosa are able to identify potential anorectics and refer them to psychological services early in the onset of the disorder and increase the likelihood of a more favorable prognosis.

3

Experiences of a Female Anorexic

Mackenzie Stroh and John Searles

Mackenzie Stroh is a recovered anorexic. John Searles is an editor for Cosmopolitan *magazine.*

Mackenzie Stroh nearly lost her life to anorexia. In the following selection, she describes her struggle with anorexia, which she traces back to when she was three years old. At that time, her parents were getting divorced and she somehow felt responsible. The divorce, combined with her inherent sensitivity and insecurity, triggered extreme compulsive behavior. Her obsession for control and perfectionism eventually lead Mackenzie to anorexia. After years of self-torture and anguish, she was successfully treated at the Montreux Clinic in Victoria, Canada, and now lives a normal and fulfilling life as an artist.

No one would ever guess from looking at me—a healthy 26-year-old artist living in Vancouver, British Columbia—that 10 years ago I almost lost my life to anorexia. I no longer weigh myself, but I'm probably around 120 pounds, an average weight for 5 feet 3 inches tall. At my lowest point, in March 1987, I weighed 65 pounds and doctors said my heart could stop at any moment. Still, the more weight I lost, the more triumphant I felt.

My deadly relationship with food goes all the way back to my childhood in Alberta, Canada. When I was 3 years old, my parents divorced. My mother moved to an apartment with my newborn brother, Jason, my 6-year-old sister, Jodie, and me. Confused and hurt by the divorce, I felt that I had to be perfect to make things easier for my family. As far back as third grade, I stayed up late doing homework while my siblings slept. I cleaned obsessively—emptying ashtrays, washing dishes. But no matter how much I tried to make myself and the world around me perfect, I felt that I fell short.

In school, people sometimes teased me that I was a "big" girl. At 4 feet and 75 pounds, I was actually quite small. I realize now that they

Excerpted from Mackenzie Stroh and John Searles, "Anorexia: Eating Disorder Investigation," *Cosmopolitan*, October 1997. Reprinted with permission from John Searles.

were being sarcastic, but their teasing—combined with my sensitivity, perfectionism, and confusion about my parents' divorce—was a recipe for an eating disorder. A voice inside my head began to whisper, "You're worthless and don't deserve food." While my brother and sister munched on cookies, I ate mostly carrots, celery, and crackers. Still, my inner voice said, "You are fat."

I first realized I had a problem at a friend's slumber party when I was about 13. Even though it was raining outside, a voice in my head told me, "You have to exercise now." I snuck away and pedaled my bike up a hilly path for an hour. When I returned soaking wet, I looked at my friends—all dry and happy—and felt very alone.

Since I was incredibly driven in both school and sports, my mother just thought of me as ambitious. She didn't realize that I compulsively rode my bike 30 miles a day and spent hours doing leg lifts and sit-ups. She also did not know that I had memorized the number of calories in almost every food, from a bowl of rice to a single banana to a handful of grapes. By the time I was 15, I had cut out all food except empty pita pockets and yogurt. I told myself I wanted to feel fit and strong, but at 5 feet 3 inches and 90 pounds, I was far from healthy. I think my family knew my low weight wasn't normal, but my habits had been part of my personality for as long as anyone could remember, so they never said anything.

My deadly relationship with food goes all the way back to my childhood in Alberta, Canada.

Outside of my family, though, people began to notice. Once, a friend's aunt took us to McDonald's—an anorexic's worst nightmare. When I said I wasn't hungry, she yelled, "You are going to eat, because I won't watch you do this to yourself!" But even as I chewed the fries that they forced me to eat, I only thought of the exercise needed to burn the 300 calories. In school, girls I barely knew said, "You're so skinny. What's wrong with you?" When guys asked me out—not often, because my fragile appearance was usually found unattractive—I always said no. I hated my "fat" body so much that I felt I was unworthy of affection. To conceal my physical self, I began to wear baggy clothes. Down to 86 pounds, I could only find clothes that fit me in the children's section at the department store. Kids pointed and sales clerks whispered as I stood in line with my children's size 10 dresses. But my embarrassment wasn't enough to quell the voice inside my head that taunted, "You need to be smaller."

The wrong treatment

When I was in the 11th grade, a 17-year-old girl came to my school to give a talk about eating disorders. Instead of finding comfort from hearing a story so similar to my own, I felt ashamed and left the room crying. But after I wiped my tears, I remembered the name of the girl's treatment facility. Without telling anyone, I made an appointment there. My heart was pounding hard inside my frail body when I showed up at the facility a few days later. The woman in charge of the facility terrified me. "Unless you come to this clinic right away," she said, "you are going to die."

In October 1986, with my family's support, I quit school to attend treatment at the center—a new age outpatient facility in Calgary. People there talked about chakras and the mind-body connection but never about food—except once, when a counselor said I should eat alfalfa sprouts for "electrolytes"! Another counselor told me to buy a bathing suit to see how bad I looked in it. This advice was useless, because I didn't care about electrolytes and I already knew how bad my body looked. In my six months at the clinic, my weight actually dropped to a dangerous 65 pounds. The counselors must have noticed. I don't think they said anything because they didn't really know how to treat anorexia.

A few weeks later, all the hair on my head fell out, and my body grew a coat of ducklinglike fur called lanugo to keep me warm—a natural reaction to extreme weight loss and common among anorexics. With so little flesh on my body, I felt chilled all the time. I took several hot baths a day to raise my body temperature. I used to lie in the tub—my mind foggy from lack of nutrients—and think about how I had failed my family. The solution sounded simple: open my mouth and eat! But the voice in my head was stronger than ever, whispering, "You are a horrible person who is torturing her family. Each pound you shed is a victory because there is less of you." Every time I stepped on the scale, I hoped to be another pound closer to death. Looking back, I realize I was trying to make myself disappear—slowly and painfully. Other methods of suicide didn't occur to me, because at the time I wasn't completely conscious of my irrational desire to disappear, to die.

I don't know the exact reason why I felt such intense self-hatred for so many years.

At home, while everyone slept, I took a bag of popcorn hidden in my closet and allowed myself a few small handfuls. I snuck down to the basement and rode the exercise bike for hours—sometimes pedaling until I blacked out. One morning, I woke up with my sister, Jodie, standing over me and crying. My head must have hit the concrete post, because there was blood all over me.

After that, my family wouldn't let me go back to the center. They took me to our family doctor, who said my heart might stop at any moment if I didn't put on weight. My mother threatened to take me to the hospital and have me hooked up to a feeding tube if I lost even one more pound. She cooked foods I was willing to nibble, like asparagus and broccoli. It took everything I had to ignore the negative voice in my head, but once or twice a day, I quickly shoved food in my mouth—10 pieces of toast, or five bowls of cereal, or three plates of vegetables—before the voice could talk me out of it.

After seven months, I was up to 115 pounds and my hair grew back. (It was a little thinner and a weird orange color before it turned back to the original dark brown three months later.) People think if an anorexic gains weight, she is cured. But even though I looked healthier, I still struggled with cruel voices in my head that chanted, "You are a failure." And the new meat on my body made me feel fat and disgusting all the time. Every day, I hated myself more.

One night, my stepmother, Georgia, went to hear a lecture by an anorexia counselor named Peggy Claude-Pierre. At the time, Peggy had only a tiny office nine hours away in Victoria [British Columbia], with no staff and a long waiting list of patients. But Georgia convinced her to see me. In the two years since I had attended the clinic in Calgary, I had seen dozens of doctors and therapists. Some said they simply couldn't help me; others prescribed fatty diets that I refused to eat. Figuring Peggy was my last chance, I agreed to meet her.

The anorexia answer

When I showed up in Peggy's office in September 1990 weighing 107 pounds, I gave her an ultimatum: "If you don't help me, I am going to kill myself." Peggy said, "I understand what's going on inside your head and we will change this together." I found an apartment nearby and a job. Fortunately, my family made all the financial arrangements.

Peggy and I met almost daily—sometimes for five minutes, sometimes for hours. "I am always here to listen to you," she told me. Even when I paged her late at night, she would call back to listen. She tried to point out that my desire to be perfect, triggered in part by my parents' divorce (my subconscious thinking went something like "if I had been a more perfect student, daughter, athlete, etc., my parents would be together"), had propelled me into a negative mind-set. Of course, no one could be perfect and my "failure" led to a downward spiral of self-loathing.

Peggy encouraged me to eat small meals throughout the day. I resisted for seven months, eating a muffin at breakfast and popcorn or salad at dinner. My weight hovered at 100 pounds. Frustrated, I often ran out of her office screaming, "You don't know what you're talking about!" Peggy would follow me and take me in her arms, saying, "You're going to get better. You are a beautiful young woman. You can do anything." Peggy's unconditional caring finally broke through. By focusing on my mind as well as my body, she helped me realize my self-doubt was normal but the way I handled it was not. Instead of torturing myself, I needed to nurture my body and spirit. I began eating bagels and bran muffins, then salads at lunch as well as dinner. At first, I felt nervous and hesitant when I ate, but the old voice had faded and a new voice told me, "You deserve to eat."

After two years of therapy with Peggy—while working and making new friends—I felt happy and healthy for the first time in my life. I was 21, and Peggy encouraged me to travel on my own. I went to Europe for four months, and when I returned home, I enrolled in art school. My creativity flourished in photo-based multimedia artwork, and I met a wonderful guy named Chris, an art director at a Canadian magazine. We've been dating for two years now and are really in love.

I don't know the exact reason why I felt such intense self-hatred for so many years. I do know that sensitivity, perfectionism, altruism, and insecurity are common characteristics among anorexics. Perhaps my desire to please my parents after their divorce, combined with those traits, created my condition. And without the caring treatment of Peggy, I never would have overcome the voices in my head.

Experiences of
a Male Anorexic

Michael Krasnow

Michael Krasnow is an anorexic and the author of My Life as a Male
Anorexic.

Michael Krasnow began his ongoing struggle with anorexia in the
mid-1980s. In the following selection from his book *My Life as a
Male Anorexic,* Krasnow describes the onset of the disease that has
affected his life for many years. According to Krasnow, he began
feeling fat when he was eleven years old but did not become
anorexic until he was a teenager. During his first year of high
school, Krasnow relates, he became depressed and developed an
obsession with studying. This obsession was eventually replaced
with an obsession about his weight. The control he gained over
his eating patterns and his food intake made him feel special and
all-powerful, Krasnow now confides.

For some time now, my mother has been encouraging me to write a
book about my screwed-up life and my experiences with anorexia nervosa and depression. I've never given this idea much consideration. Because of the depression, I just haven't had the motivation. However, now
that I'm not working, I figure I may as well give it a shot. After all, it's
been around two years since I stopped working; most of this time has
been spent sitting in a chair in my apartment, staring at the wall. Talk
about a waste. These past couple of years epitomize my life—a total waste.

First, the facts that make me an "official" anorexic. The so-called professionals, your $100-per-hour, know-it-all doctors, will list many symp-
toms and characteristics of anorexia. The bottom line is that I am 5'9"
and feel fat, despite weighing only 75 pounds. Just for the record, I am
white, American, Jewish, and twenty-five years old. I live in Hollywood,
Florida, and . . . my name is Michael Krasnow. What sets me aside from
most other anorexics is that I am male.

For years, anorexia existed, but very few people knew of it. Women
who suffered from it did not realize that they were not alone. Eventually,

as more became known and anorexia became more publicized, a greater number of women came forward to seek help, no longer feeling that they would be considered strange or outcasts from society. Maybe with the publication of this book, more men with the problem will realize that they are not alone either, and that they do not suffer from a "woman's disease." They can come forward without worrying about embarrassment.

Who knows? Maybe as a result of this book, I'll end up on television. . . . The more publicity I can get, the better. Each book that is sold will make that many more people aware of the serious problem of male anorexia. And the more people that know, the more demand there will be to help those with this problem. . . .

So much for preliminaries. It is time to tell you about myself. . . .

Feelings of being fat

I suppose I had a typical childhood. Born in Rochester, New York, on April 27, 1969, I moved to Framingham, Massachusetts, when I was two months old and lived there for about twenty-two years. I enjoyed being with my friends and family, loved to read and play sports, had a hobby (comic books) and a newspaper route, watched TV, idolized Larry Bird and the Boston Celtics, and had no worries. I was an all-around average child. My one unusual characteristic was that I felt fat from as early as age eleven, when I was in the sixth grade. I occasionally mentioned this feeling to my parents and grandparents, but not with any seriousness. I used to joke with them that I was going to diet. Understandably, no one paid any attention. After all, I was of average weight. Actually, I was less than average, the type of child that others refer to as "so skinny."

When I speak of feeling fat, what I mean is that when I look down at my stomach, I see it as sticking out or being bloated. . . .

I started to wonder why I felt fat. I knew that statistically I wasn't fat, and everyone told me how skinny I was. I decided to try dieting, but never kept to it for more than a couple of days (I figured it was a lack of willpower). Because I never stuck to a diet, no one paid much attention.

At this time, my feelings of being fat began to affect my activities. Before, I had felt fat, but had not been influenced by these feelings. Now, I would not go to the beach because I did not want to take off my shirt. Without a shirt, I'd see my stomach and feel fat; I believed others who saw my stomach would also think I looked fat. When I could not make up an excuse for not going to the beach, I kept my shirt on, or if I had to take it off, I sucked in my gut and held it.

Without a shirt, I'd see my stomach and feel fat.

Sucking in my gut became a way of life. I played basketball in my temple's youth league. In practice, we scrimmaged as "shirts" and "skins." I hated being on the "skins" team. When I was, I was unable to focus on the game, being too preoccupied with thinking about sucking in my gut. . . .

My father was a member of a health club, Racquetball Five-O. . . . I went to this health club with my dad once or twice a week. When I was in the locker room, naked, I always sucked in my gut.

I am singling out these locker-room occasions because they lead to an interesting observation. Standing in that locker room, I saw the other men around me as being fat. In other words, I felt fat, but my disillusionment was not limited to myself. Most anorexics will see other people as being thin. I'm different; I also view other people as being fat, even if they aren't. If someone says that so-and-so is thin, I will frequently think otherwise. . . .

Depression and obsessive studying

It was at the start of my first year in high school, September 1983, that my "fat feelings" gained strength, and my troubles started. Oddly, it was strange behavior of a different sort that preceded the anorexia. As a freshman, I became obsessed with studying. . . .

On the very first day of school, I signed up to run on the cross-country track team. I was an okay runner. I improved a lot after that first day.

In the middle of October, my grandfather died after suffering from cancer for about two years. . . . It's true that his death coincided with the time that my depression and obsessive studying began, but as far as I'm concerned, it was just coincidence.

When the depression began, I quit the cross-country track team. I simply did not have the motivation. A month later, I tried out for and made the freshman basketball team. I sat on the bench 99 percent of the time and after about one month, my depression increased and the studying began to get out of hand. I quit basketball (I had already given up my newspaper route) and began to devote all my time to my school work.

I also view other people as being fat, even if they aren't.

I got home from school about 2:30 in the afternoon and studied until midnight. Soon, I was studying until 1:00 in the morning—then 2:00. Eventually, I started going to bed at 2:00 A.M. and setting my alarm for 4:00 A.M., so that I could study some more before school. I even studied on the fifteen-minute bus ride to school. . . .

The studying was probably part obsession, part perfection. Every piece of homework had to be immaculate. For instance, my math homework could not have one little erasure mark. This meant I might have to copy it over four, five, or six times. This perfection was very frustrating. To vent this frustration, I began banging my head against the wall. . . .

During these few months that my studying and depression worsened, I began to see a psychiatrist, Dr. C. . . .

Dr. C prescribed antidepressant medication. From 1984 until 1990, I was on and off different antidepressants (nortriptyline, imipramine, desipramine, amoxapine, amitriptyline, and Prozac). Since none of these ever helped or made any difference, there is no point in discussing each time I began a new one. . . .

My parents and Dr. C decided to withdraw me from school. They made the right decision. Deep down, I think I wanted this to happen. By being out of school, I did not have the need to study. There was nothing I could do about it. Because I had no control over the matter, I would not feel guilty for not studying. Once I was out of school, it was out of my hands. . . .

A new obsession

When he took me out of school, Dr. C said that he had one main concern. He was worried that I would replace my obsession with studying with a new obsession. This possibility had never occurred to me until he mentioned it. Dr. C put the idea of a new obsession into my mind. As a result, when I left school, I found myself thinking, "Okay, Dr. C said I might end up with a new obsession; now, what can I do to replace the studying?" In other words, I made a conscious effort to find a new obsession. To this day, although I could be wrong, I truly believe that this would not have happened if Dr. C had not said anything.

What was this new obsession? It was toothbrushing. At first, I was brushing about two hours per day. Very soon, it was twelve hours per day. While either sitting in front of the television or walking around the house, I would brush, brush, brush. This lasted for only a couple of weeks (I went through a lot of toothpaste and a lot of toothbrushes), before I made the decision that would lead to the anorexia.

I really hated the toothbrushing. Who wouldn't? One day, I woke up and said to myself, "Oh, gee, I don't want to brush my teeth all day. Well, hey, don't have anything to eat, your mouth won't get dirty, and you won't have to brush." With this in mind, I didn't eat that day. I also did not eat (I did drink water) for the next three days.

Of course, Dr. C and my parents became extremely worried about my physical well-being. Finally, on June 16, 1984, I was admitted to Westwood Lodge, a psychiatric hospital in Westwood, Massachusetts. . . .

Upon being admitted, I was assigned to Dr. B. He was now the boss. I was through with Dr. C. I still refused to have anything but water. My vital signs became very bad. My blood pressure was so low that the nurse had trouble taking it. My temperature was below 96 degrees. . . .

My feelings about the hospital were similar to those I had when I was taken out of school. Deep down, I think that I wanted to be hospitalized. It was a relief. Again, it was a control issue. I had to eat—I thought I had no choice (in later years, I would realize that I had more control than I thought), but I couldn't brush my teeth more than the allotted fifteen minutes. I would not feel guilty for not brushing because I had no control over it.

After a few weeks, the toothbrushing was no longer a problem. There was really no explanation for this. I think it was simply a matter of "out of sight, out of mind.". . .

Focusing on anorexia

How does everything I've been telling you about Westwood and the toothbrushing relate to the anorexia? Well, as you know, I'd been feeling fat for years, but never believed that I had the willpower to diet. Now, I saw that I did. The anorexia became the focus of my life.

I always believed that feeling fat was something I couldn't help. This was no longer the case. There was something I could do about it. I had the willpower to diet. I was all-powerful Michael. No longer would I feel fat and put up with it. Instead, I would do something or hate myself. Except for my family, Dr. B was the first person to whom I ever mentioned feeling fat. When I did this, he told me it was a characteristic of anorexia nervosa. "What's that?" I asked. When he explained the condition, I automatically labeled myself an anorexic. It's hard to explain, but it almost seemed "glamorous" to me (I don't know if that's the right word), something I wanted. I had an illness; I had something few others had; I was special. The anorexia gave me an identity and made me an individual.

It was at Westwood that I first became focused on the weight (number of pounds) itself. At one point, I was weighing myself hourly or every other hour. This did not last long. There was no point in constant weight checking. There would be basically no change.

The first way I noticed a difference in my weight was that my clothes felt loose. This made me feel *so* good. For the next five or six years, whenever I would be losing weight, I would get a "high" by getting dressed in the morning, and feeling that my pants had become that much bigger on me.

I always believed that feeling fat was something I couldn't help.

After being at Westwood for two months, my insurance ran out. There was really no reason for me not to go home. The toothbrushing wasn't a problem, and although I thought of losing weight, this had not yet become a serious issue. However, Dr. B and I did have one concern about my going home. It was mid-August, about three weeks before the start of school. We feared that in an unstructured environment, with a lot of free time on my hands, I would fall back into the habit of brushing my teeth. Because of this, it was decided that I would be transferred to the psychiatric ward of Norwood Hospital, a medical facility in Norwood, Massachusetts. (Insurance would not cover my stay at a private psychiatric hospital, but it would cover my stay on a psychiatric ward of a medical hospital.) I would stay there for about two weeks and go home one week before school started. This week would give me time to get back into the flow of everyday life outside the hospital.

In essence, Norwood was just "temporary housing" for me, noteworthy for only one reason. It was here that I had my first feelings of competition. There were one or two other anorexics (there had been none at Westwood). I felt that I had to be the skinniest, lose more weight than anyone else, and have the strictest guidelines around what I did or did not eat. These feelings were not strong, nor did I act on them. However, they were there.

Back to school

When I returned home from the hospital the last week in August 1984, I did not keep the anorexia a secret. When I had left school in April, I had said that it was because of mononucleosis. At the time, the other students knew that I studied a lot, but they did not know to what degree. The idea of seeing a psychiatrist, and later of being in a psychiatric hospital, had embarrassed me. I now knew that there was no reason for this embarrassment. Others could accept me as I was or shun me. It was their choice. . . .

Before my discharge from Westwood, Dr. B, my parents, and I had set a program I was to follow outside of the hospital. I needed to maintain my weight at 120 pounds, which was what it had been during my hospitalization. (I don't remember how much I had weighed before the hospital—maybe around 135.) Anything less would put me in serious medical danger and require rehospitalization, perhaps even tube feeding. This is a perfect example of why I now ignore doctors and believe that half the time, they don't know what they're talking about. Anything less than 120 pounds would be medically dangerous, and yet here I am today, not in great shape but functioning okay, at 75 pounds. . . .

On my first day back at school, I once again signed up for the cross-country track team. This would be my extracurricular activity. However, two days later, I quit. I was still depressed and just didn't have the motivation. Instead of a school-related activity, I got a part-time job. I worked approximately ten hours a week in the public library as a library page.

For the first few months of school, which were from September 1984 until the beginning of 1985, things remained basically the same. I was seeing [a new psychiatrist], Dr. P, two times a week and sticking to the agreement I had made upon leaving Westwood. Around the beginning of 1985, things began to go downhill.

My depression led to a lack of interest in socializing and other people. Soon, I had no friends and no social life. Some of my old friends remained faithful and let it be known that they would always be there for me, but I didn't really care.

I lost five pounds, going down to 115. . . .

Five unusual habits

In addition to the continuous depression, which had increased since my return to school, and the weight loss, I developed some unusual habits, which I still follow. The five most prevalent were (1) refusal to eat any low-calorie or diet foods, (2) refusal to let anyone see me eat, (3) constant wearing of jacket or bathrobes, (4) refusal to drink water, and (5) refusal to swallow my saliva.

(1) *Refusal to eat any low-calorie or diet foods.* I don't know if they are right, but this, along with the refusal to drink water, is a characteristic of mine that has led various therapists to label me as one of the most severe anorexics they have ever encountered. Many anorexics will allow themselves to fill up on low-calorie foods (diet sodas, salads, etc.), so that they will not be hungry. To me, this demonstrates a lack of willpower. I will not let myself fill up on these foods. Abstinence is the key to my feelings of self-control and being all-powerful almost as though restricting my intake is a challenge.

(2) *Refusal to let anyone see me eat.* Aside from my mother and brother, I will not eat in front of anyone. I first became uneasy in the school cafeteria. I felt that the other students were watching me, as if I were a pig. I started thinking, "Gee, they're probably wondering what I'm doing with

food. After all, I have anorexia—I'm not supposed to eat." It was probably my imagination; they most likely never even noticed me. Odds are, none of them could have cared less. Still, I was uncomfortable and decided from then on to have my lunch in the bathroom, a private cubicle in the library, or anywhere else I wouldn't be seen. This carried over into my house. If we had guests, they did not see me eat.

My parents did not know how to deal with me or even what to think.

---

(3) *Constant wearing of jacket or bathrobes.* Because I feel fat whenever I look at myself, I always wear a jacket in public to cover up my stomach. I don't mean occasionally, but almost all the time. When I am home, I will wear two bathrobes instead of the jacket, taking them off only when I go to bed or shower. I know that when I was in school, some of the students considered me strange because of my depression and unsociability. I don't know what they thought of my constant need to wear a jacket, but it probably added to my "weird" image. With one or two exceptions, since graduation, I haven't seen any of the kids from school. Maybe some of them are reading this book right now, thinking, "I remember that loser. So that's why he never took off his coat."

(4) *Refusal to drink water.* I do not drink water—I mean never. I have not had any water since February 1985. Now, I know there is water in everything. What I mean by no water is that I will not drink plain water; I will not go to a sink, pour myself some water, and drink it. This coincides with what I said earlier about my refusal to have any low-calorie or diet foods. The abstinence from water is almost like a challenge. I know water has no calories, but I would still feel fat if I drank it.

I remember the day I decided to stop drinking water. I had worked at the library from six in the evening until nine. I got home about fifteen minutes later, and ran to the sink to gulp down a few glasses of water. This was something I frequently did. With my dry mouth, a side effect of antidepressant medication and a result of limited intake, I was usually thirsty. After I had the water, I lifted my shirt, looked at my stomach, and felt so fat. I saw my stomach as sticking out, immensely bloated. I decided right then and there that I would never again drink water. If I was thirsty, that would be my tough luck. Talk about willpower. I have not had a drink of water since.

(5) *Refusal to swallow my saliva.* In March, a month after I stopped having water, I decided not to swallow my saliva. This is stupid, you say? I know. I agree. But, it's the way I am. I constantly spit out my saliva. To do this, I always have a paper cup or a paper towel in my jacket pocket. I spit into these twenty-four hours per day. Even when I go to sleep in the evening, I keep one or the other by my side.

False hopes

Let me tell you a bit about Dr. P. Dr. B recommended him at the time of my discharge from Westwood Lodge. I saw Dr. P two times a week; each session lasted fifty minutes. For the first few months, I looked forward to our meetings. I wanted to get better and was willing to do anything. I guess I still thought of doctors as being miracle workers. This soon changed with Dr. P. . . .

What were our sessions like? Well, a typical session would start with each of us saying hello. Then we would sit down and look at each other. After doing this for fifty minutes, he would tell me that my time was up, and I would leave. This is the truth. I'm serious. He was getting paid around sixty dollars per hour, and we were staring at each other. That's all. No talking. I think I even occasionally dozed off (sixty dollars is an expensive nap).

In all, I saw Dr. P for almost two and a half years; our sessions came to an end when he moved to another state. During this time, my depression increased to the point where it could not get any worse. It never let up. I just wanted to die.

I frequently told my parents that I wanted to stop seeing Dr. P. He did not help and was a complete waste of time. I could be wrong, but I believe he was more interested in money than anything else (either that, or he was totally incompetent).

Because I felt that Dr. P was not helping, my parents sought the advice of Dr. B and other doctors whom they knew. However, all these doctors recommended that I continue to see Dr. P, and therefore, I did. Although I had become more depressed and lost a little weight, my parents did not know what else to do. Perhaps they feared that if I stopped seeing Dr. P, I would "fall apart." My parents were doing what they thought was best, maybe entertaining some false hope about what I could get out of these doctor appointments.

Males are anorexics, too

Although concern about anorexia is growing, there is still a large unawareness, especially about male anorexia, and this is the major purpose of my story—so that other men with this problem will realize that they are not alone. My parents and I could not pick up a book and read about male anorexics. For all we knew, I was the only man in the world with anorexia. My parents did not know how to deal with me or even what to think. We had no one to whom we could turn. Perhaps if a book like this one had been around at the time, things would have been different.

5

Anorexia Is Caused by a Destructive Drive for Perfection

Peggy Claude-Pierre

Peggy Claude-Pierre is the founder of the Montreux Clinic, a residential inpatient program specializing in eating disorders. She consults with health professionals all over the world on eating disorders.

Many experts believe that anorexia is caused by a number of factors including dysfunctional parents and family life, physical and sexual abuse, and societal expectations for body size. However, these factors only trigger anorexic behavior in individuals who are predisposed to self-destructive behavior. The real cause of anorexia is the Negative Mind and Confirmed Negativity Condition (CNC). An individual develops CNC early in life and later expresses it in many obsessive and destructive behaviors, including anorexia and other eating disorders. With CNC, a person harbors a strong self-hatred, strives for unattainable perfection, and does not feel worthy to live. This emotion manifests itself through destructive behavior like self-starvation. The only way to successfully treat an anorexic is to reverse CNC.

"I have always been told I am a controlling perfectionist."

"I can't be cured. I'm too bad. I'm going to have to deal with this the rest of my life. I just have to live with it."

"It's those pictures of supermodels in the magazines that put Jamie on this incessant diet."

"They told me my daughter is going to be released on Sunday. She's only sixteen. Her insurance has run out. They told me to prepare for her death. There is nothing more they can do."

"I don't deserve to get well. I feel so dirty, hopeless, no-good, fat, scared, a failure, insecure. I really don't deserve to live."

"I am disgusted with myself for being the cause of all this."

"My daughter is 5 feet 8 inches and sixty pounds. There's not much left of her. She won't comply with anyone. She's only been out of hospitals for two four-month periods in the last three years. She has ruined the family."

"My husband and I aren't speaking. We don't really have a relationship anymore. My kids hate me for ignoring them because my own problems were more important than they were. I've tried; can you help? It's been almost a dozen years. Our home is a war zone and my therapist refuses to see me anymore because I lost too much weight and didn't stick to the bargains we made."

"They say I am selfish; that all I care about is how I look."

"My doctor told me I don't want to grow up."

"I am the worst case they have ever seen and I'm incurable."

"She refuses to deal with her underlying issues no matter how many psychiatrists she sees."

"I used to be the perfect child with everything going for me, but I have lost it all!"

"I'm not worth saving, but I might prove an interesting experiment."

"I don't want my daughter to die. They say we are a dysfunctional family, but my wife and I are still together. We don't fight and we love our daughter very much. They say they can do no more for my daughter. She is only nineteen. It is not the natural order of things that she should die first. Surely something can be done."

Taken to their extreme, eating disorders are, after all, a slow form of suicide.

All of these statements are based on myths and misconceptions about anorexia and bulimia. Unfortunately, many of these myths still hold sway today and are often the basis upon which we regard and treat patients with eating disorders.

I hope to offer an alternative to these myths and set in their place what I have perceived is the true nature of eating disorders—CNC [Confirmed Negativity Condition] and the Negative Mind.

Myth: Anorexia is a by-product of our culture

A widely held theory expounds that anorexia is in part caused by a culture that values appearance over substance and prizes women only when they are thin. Much has been said about the cult of thinness, the rise of the supermodel as a public icon, and the belief that victims of eating disorders lose weight to emulate a supposed physical ideal.

Eating disorders are eight times more common in women than in men. Surely one of the external values society offers as venue of perfection is the female body. Women grow up being complimented more on their looks than on any other quality. We are told that most women are perpetually dieting. Yet we must be careful about assessing blame for eating disorders to this aspect of contemporary society without considering the broader context.

The deification of thinness is dangerous, but where eating disorders are concerned, it can be misleading. Indeed, this is a much more complicated issue than appears at first glance, and if a connection exists between the cult of thinness and anorexia, it is far deeper than mere vanity.

There is a difference between becoming thin for the sake of fitting into society's expectations and becoming thinner and thinner and thinner for the sake of dying. Taken to their extreme, eating disorders are, after all, a slow form of suicide.

If models in their beauteous, supposed perfection are an example to the vulnerable, why do those suffering eating disorders progress so far beyond thinness to emaciation and, ultimately, death? Why are boys and men affected? Why will one model become anorexic and another not? Why do elderly women become anorexics crippled with arthritis? Why do small children?

The distorted perception starts early—I have counseled patients as young as three years old—and I now believe that the "failure to thrive" cited in infants can be in some instances an early manifestation of the Negative Mind. The seeds of anorexia may have been planted at a much earlier age than the one at which individuals become body-conscious.

Society's emphasis on looks clouds the more important issue that children are dying because they are trying to achieve impossible standards of perfection. This focus on perfection is not so much for personal gratification as it is a misguided attempt to improve the world.

Anorexia is about self-loathing and self-hatred for falling short of perfection.

Rather than thinking of the supermodel syndrome as a cause of eating disorders, it is best to think of it as a possible trigger. Modeling is an area in which perfection seems attainable, one of the many venues for perfection (such as sports, academics, dance, and so on) that eating disorder victims will fit themselves into. Most teenage girls try to lose a few pounds for the sake of attracting boys in high school. Many women are constantly on a diet, unhappy with their bodies. But a girl with an eating disorder will use the ideal of the model as a way to hone her sense of perfection; boys are not on her mind. A woman with an eating disorder doesn't want to be a size 6; she wants to be a size 0. The difference is knowing how much of what society presents to take seriously.

I do believe that media and advertising images that glorify perfection and beauty contribute to many women's sense of unhappiness about their imperfectly human bodies. I would applaud a movement to curtail the supermodel syndrome. But I am not convinced that the rate of eating disorders would fall as a result; I believe that people with CNC would find another venue of perfection to emulate.

Moreover, anorexics frequently suffer from gross distortion of their body image. They will often claim they are overweight in the face of all physical evidence to the contrary. One young woman planning a third suicide attempt wrote to me that, at five foot four, she weighed 93 pounds. "I feel fat all the time," she said, "but before I kill myself, I must be thin. I cannot let some undertaker see my ugly fat body."

The DSM-IV, the latest diagnostic manual of psychiatric conditions, states, "Individuals with this disorder intensely fear gaining weight or becoming fat. This intense fear of becoming fat is usually not alleviated by the weight loss. In fact, concern about weight gain often increases even as actual weight continues to decrease."

I believe that the Negative Mind will not allow its victims to see themselves as they are because weight is synonymous with life. Given that victims are on an unconscious track to total self-negation (death), if they perceive themselves as fat, this will allow the Negative Mind to demand that they lose even more weight.

Anorexics will lie about whether they have eaten because of the Negative Mind, which insists without reason or logic on their demise, instructs them to. They wear concealing clothes to protect the Negative Mind, to forestall confrontation with the people around them. In the few cases in which anorexics flaunt their gauntness, they are pointing out that they are more unworthy than others. They vie to be the best at dying.

Anorexia is about self-loathing and self-hatred for falling short of perfection. Nora wrote several years after her recovery, "I didn't look at models and dream of looking like them. I didn't think that I was becoming beautiful. I thought I was the ugliest, most selfish, and horrible person."

Anorexia in males

I do agree that women are bombarded with images of unattainable female beauty. Women's magazines are filled with articles and advertisements touting diets, weight loss, exercise machines, and so on. Beautiful women are featured in television ads that sell everything from beer to automobiles to detergent.

Though the images of "perfect" women still vastly outnumber those extolling male perfection, I do in fact see a rise in the number of images of men, although they are perhaps more obscured. *Men's Health* and *GQ* as opposed to *Glamour* and *Vogue*—the magazine titles may not always be as direct.

Once again, however, I think we are looking at a trigger, not a direct cause. Eating disorders are not gender-based any more than CNC is gender-based.

Historically, women have been honed to be the caregivers of home and therefore of society's needs. For years, they have been the quiet support person, the one to whom the expressions "The power behind the throne" and "Behind every great man is a great woman" applied. So naturally, it would follow that there would be a higher incidence of eating disorder manifestation among females.

Today, society is evolving. Men can act more sensitively. We are finally a more humanistic culture rather than a culture of warriors.

And eating disorders among men are on the rise—at least one million men number among the eight million people afflicted with them in the United States. I attribute this to the ever-increasing anxiety and attitudes toward perceived stress in society (the macrocosm) and the changing rules within the nuclear family (the microcosm), coupled with the victim's sensitive, caring nature.

Perhaps men are not faced with the anxiety of society's contradictions as often because their stereotypical role is to do rather than to mediate and placate. But given the changing roles in society, men see themselves more often in the position of giving care. One young man who came into my care after years of hospitalization that culminated in institutionalization in a mental facility because of the severity of his suicidality had begun his slide toward CNC and anorexia as a young boy. His mother had suffered stomach problems so intense that she had to run to the hospital for treatment. Jonathan took it upon himself to keep his two younger siblings quiet while his mother recovered from her frequent ailments. She had not asked him to do this, but in his own mind, he saw it as his role.

Each case of anorexia is different.

Each case of anorexia is different. But anorexics all hear the same language and display the same inherent kindness. After their recovery, their Actual Minds will regain control, and these former victims will be objectively, not subjectively, kind.

Myth: Anorexia is caused by abuse

Abuse falls into the category of "Underlying Issues." These issues are real, and they need to be addressed. In this discussion, I applaud the work being done with people who have such issues. At the same time, however, I question whether these issues are directly related to anorexia. As one victim wrote to me, "I don't know how to change. Any program I've been in was a stop-gap measure—a one- or three-month hospital stay where I'd put on weight that I'd immediately drop as soon as I was released. (Sure, I worked through many important issues—but never unraveled the behavior.)"

I keep reading that eating disorders are skyrocketing because sexual abuse is coming out of the closet. I have had patients come to me and say, "I don't remember being sexually abused, but since I have anorexia, I guess I must have been."

I know of one father who was accused of sexually abusing his daughter because she was anorexic. There was no evidence for believing he had molested his little girl. Even though no one in the family could see how this abuse was possible, the mother divorced him because of the groundless charge. Both child and father denied any abuse took place, and I believe them—it took me two years to put the family back together.

I do not deny that sexual abuse occurs in situations in which child and parent vigorously deny it, nor do I want to minimize the devastating trauma that can occur after sexual abuse. However, most of my patients have not been abused, and I want to set aside the common misconception that every eating disorder is the product of abuse—physical, sexual, or otherwise.

On the other hand, I have worked with several anorexics who have been sexually abused. They felt that they deserved what happened to them, they did not feel traumatized by it, and were primarily relieved that it had not occurred to someone else. Typically, they welcomed what must seem to the rest of us like cruel punishment (the work of the ever-perverse Negative Mind), and still they cared for others first—even their abusers. In truth, they lacked an accurate perception of their reality and responsibility.

Consequently, I believe it may not be the trauma of the abuse per se, but the individual's perception of reality that will cause anorexia. We can change reality only to a certain point (by addressing the trauma and distress that act as triggers), but we can try to change people's attitudes toward and perceptions of reality. In other words, we can objectify abuse, that is, try to help the abused victim understand that she did not deserve or cause the abuse, in order to preserve the sanity of the victim. Perhaps anger toward ignorance only compounds the problem and prolongs the suffering of the victim. Compassion and understanding for the limitations of human awareness would seem more likely to heal the victim than criticizing her for not condemning her abuse or her abuser.

Myth: Anorexia is caused by dysfunctional parents

There is a widespread perception that anorexia is more common in families in which rigid, exacting, uncompromising parents impose their own personalities on compliant little children. The "best little girl in the world" stereotype conveys that nothing the child does is good enough for insatiable, demanding parents, so the child keeps trying harder and harder to please them.

This is blatantly untrue for the vast majority of my cases. In fact, I was alarmed to discover how wrong the stereotype is. It would have made it easier to find that parents were uncaring or demanding or dysfunctional, because then the answer to the eating disorder conundrum would have been much simpler.

Parents are primarily responsible for defining the world in which their children find themselves, but the emergence of an eating disorder is not in itself a response to a specific social structure within the family. Rather, I find that motivation for achievement is far more self-imposed.

I have observed that these children are determined to create the best possible scenario for the ones they love, without having been asked or pushed. Generally, the intense striving to achieve and the insatiable need for validation come from within them, not from external sources such as parents.

Parents are people—they are human and imperfect.

One girl wrote in her journal, "I was running track before school, doing homework instead of eating lunch, doing more running after school, studying until one o'clock or two o'clock in the morning and sleeping four or five hours a night, maximum. . . . I contemplated driving my car around a corner and not turning because I had gotten a 97 percent on a project that was worth only a fraction of my final grade. I made *one* stupid mistake on a departmental exam and it haunted me for months! Nothing was ever good enough. And when I did achieve 'perfection,' it meant nothing to me."

Another wrote, "I cannot recognize or appreciate any of my own accomplishments. Others are always better. Even when I achieve excellence it isn't good enough. I recently got 98 percent on my calculus final and was upset with myself for not doing better. My goals are far too high. I lose sight of what is realistic or even excellent, and strive for what is impossible. I never reach it, so I am always a failure in my estimation and that makes me unhappy."

Moreover, young people with eating disorders work at parenting their parents; they insist on caring for the adults. Parents are generally struck by the maturity of these children from a very early age and tend to lean on them because they can.

Most of the parents whom I see are incredible—extremely loving and caring. They are also incredibly human—they have flaws and faults like the rest of us. Parents are people—they are human and imperfect. Every family in the world has circumstances that play the scale of that humanness. Motivation and the effort to make things work are all that are available to any of us. Failure requires tolerance and understanding without one being labeled a misfit.

6

Anorexics Are Victims of Society's Obsession with Thinness

Susan Renes

Susan Renes is an eating disorders specialist and a certified relapse prevention specialist.

In our media-centered culture, we are constantly bombarded by advertisements and messages that suggest that thinness leads to happiness and fulfillment. As a result, individuals, and particularly teenagers, become obsessed with meeting these unrealistically high standards for body shape and size set by society. Ironically, those who aggressively pursue thinness in their quest for happiness are usually led to self-destruction.

In the summer of 1994, I visited Dachau, a restored concentration camp outside of Munich, Germany. The visit had a profound effect on me in many ways. I wept when I saw how the prisoners had suffered, and the terrible conditions under which they lived. It had another effect on me as well.

For 10 years, I suffered from anorexia nervosa, an eating disorder characterized by starving oneself. But refusing to eat is only a small part of the disorder. It is an oppressive illness that tears down the victim psychologically and physically. Its organizing style of oppression has many similarities to the style used by the administrators of death in the Nazi concentration camps. I am not suggesting that my suffering was comparable to the atrocities experienced by concentration camp prisoners. However, after coming to a better understanding of how they were treated, I have come to believe that all oppression, whether from within or from without, has a similar organizing style.

Emblazoned on the gate of the entrance to Dachau were the German words, "Arbeit Macht Frei." Its English translation is "Work Is Freedom," or "Work Will Set You Free." The Nazis justified their use of the concentration camps to the German people and to their victims by implying that

Reprinted, with permission, from Susan Renes, "The Tyranny of Thinness," *Professional Counselor*, August 1997. Renes can be reached at 1016 E. 8th St., Port Angeles, WA 98362-6423; phone 360-452-3087.

the prisoners had strayed from the beliefs that would make Germany more powerful. Putting them to work, they claimed, would help them "concentrate" on the rehabilitation necessary for them to become productive German citizens. Of course, we now know that their true purpose was nothing less than the annihilation of the Jews and anyone else who disagreed with their beliefs.

In our modern-day Western culture, we are bombarded by advertising and mass media messages that say women must be as thin as the models they see in magazines and on television; thin is healthy; thinness brings happiness, excitement, success, and fulfillment; women must "concentrate" and work hard in order to be thin. Men and women both drive themselves hard, sometimes compulsively, to achieve these ideals, spending hours of time and thousands of dollars. They starve themselves. They exercise for hours at a time. They disregard their need for a normal body weight and a sufficient amount of food to adequately sustain them.

Refusing to eat is only a small part of the disorder.

The direct intent of these messages is not intended to hurt people, but neither was the implication that prisoners could work to make themselves free. However, there is irony in the lies behind such statements. Both attempt to make people believe they can attain freedom and happiness, when in actuality, they result in destruction. The Nazis had an incredible system of propaganda that they used to convince the German people of the correctness of their tyrannical actions. Similarly, our teen and adult magazines, books, movies, and advertisements preach the gospel of thinness, while at the same time 50 percent of our 9-year-olds are dieting and the number of reported eating disorders has never been higher. The tyranny goes on unquestioned.

After reading books about those who had survived the concentration camps, I was more familiar with the psychological tyranny the prisoners endured. Again, the treatment by the Nazis of their prisoners was not that different from the psychological symptoms experienced by an anorexic: look for an opportunity in every situation to blame the victims; institute a systematic program to remind the individuals of their powerlessness; physically starve the victims, so that their capacity to endure the stress is diminished; humiliate and denigrate them whenever possible; require that they work themselves to exhaustion while consistently demanding standards of perfection. Isn't that what anorexics do to themselves?

The most amazing part of what I learned about Dachau during my visit was that under all that oppression from which the prisoners could not escape, secret societies were formed to work for the liberation of the camp. These societies were important in the liberation of Dachau, as they snuck information to the Allied Forces, and the camp was liberated before the Germans could respond, saving many of the prisoners' lives.

For the person suffering from an eating disorder, there is also a strong desire for the pain of the experience to stop. The support groups, the friends, the therapists, the education can all be seen as Allied Forces coming to liberate the person from the persecutors who live within.

7

Anorexics Derive a Sense of Power from Their Behavior

Georgie Binks

Georgie Binks is a writer in Toronto.

Georgie Binks began flirting with self-starvation and anorexia in her late teens. In the following selection, she describes her addiction to self-starvation and how she derives a strong sense of power from it. Binks relates that as she starves herself she becomes overwhelmed with euphoria and feels good about her body. While she acknowledges that the behavior can be dangerous and even life-threatening, she argues that she has always been able to control her eating disorder before it became a serious problem.

As far as bad habits go, if I were a pack-a-day smoker who kept falling off the wagon, I'd probably be getting friendly advice from everyone—use the patch, try hypnosis, chew this gum and if none of those worked, maybe a smoker's rights group would work.

Drink too much? Well, as long as I wasn't driving and it didn't affect my job, my friends might simply take it as an appreciation of alcohol, especially if it was good red wine that had me by the collar.

But my bad habit is one that makes everybody's eyes widen when they hear it. It is not socially acceptable, and absolutely no one has a sense of humor about it. My bad habit is that I like to starve myself from time to time. The doctors say it must be a psychological problem. Perhaps I should be looking at what I am going through when I'm depriving myself of food. But I think it is just a very effective and enjoyable form of weight loss, one that I have had control over for years now.

I think if people understood how good starving themselves feels, they would understand people with eating disorders a lot better. They would also do their best to make sure no one ever got an inkling of the feeling, because once a trip has been taken down that road, it's a difficult trip back for most people. And that's probably why, according to the National Association of Anorexia Nervosa and Associated Disorders, there are 7 million women and 1 million men who suffer from eating disorders. (They

Reprinted from Georgie Binks, "The Joys of Anorexia," *Salon.com*, January 27, 2000, at http://www.Salon.com. An online version remains in the Salon archives. Reprinted with permission from Salon.com.

report that 6 percent of all serious cases die from the disorder.) I am one of the fortunate ones, because I have always been able to stop before it became a serious problem.

I never made a conscious effort to use starving myself as a dieting tool. I was always a skinny child because I was utterly bored with food. But at 16, I discovered fast food. My first taste of a Harvey's burger was heaven. I used to lie to my parents, pushing my plate away at dinner and telling them I was off to the library, while my friends and I headed off for a cheeseburger with extra dill pickles. After a few months, we discovered a little crepe house downtown and began to frequent it without our parents' knowledge. I gained a bit of weight, but at 5-foot-7 and 107 pounds, I definitely had nothing to worry about. I had grown quickly and my weight hadn't yet caught up with me.

My bad habit is that I like to starve myself from time to time.

My first real flirtation with starving came during my second year at college. I admit that part of my problem was that I was in an up-and-down love affair. But it wasn't my first, so why would I start starving myself now and not for the other romances? At the beginning I simply didn't feel like eating. So for the first couple of days I just downed a Coke for breakfast and smoked a cigarette, the same for lunch and about a half a portion of dinner. After about three days I dubbed it the "Coke and cigarettes diet." After a month and a half I weighed 102, down from the 118 I had weighed when I arrived at the university. Cheekbones had replaced the baby fat on my face and my hipbones actually stood out. To this day, that is a memory I cherish.

However, my boyfriend (the up-and-down one) told me I looked awful and fortunately I believed him. Or if I didn't, I heeded his comments anyway and started eating. That summer I gained back the weight and the cheeks during my job as a waitress at a Rocky Mountains resort.

It was not until about 10 years later that starving myself came in handy again. This time there was more going on in my life than usual, but I don't think that was the issue. It started out with stomach jitters over a failed romance and a move to a new city. Not eating properly for a few days gave me that great "high" I remembered from the Coke and cigarettes days. That was what had hooked me then and what was doing it now. Doctors who work with anorexics say it's not unusual. People in concentration camps who are starving feel euphoric, but apparently it's a transient feeling that goes away after a while.

During this little foray into starvation land, I lived mainly on apple juice and cigarettes. I'd mellowed in my choice of beverages, but the cigarettes were still an integral part of the diet because they were so successful at killing my appetite. This time I also started an exercise program, which helped put me down two dress sizes. In addition to that, I started what I thought was bulimia, but is known as "normal weight vomiting." (It's only called bulimia if it includes bingeing followed by throwing up.) I simply ate a normal dinner and then threw it up. The only problem with this was that while it was something I initially did on my own, it eventually turned into something my body was doing whether or not I liked it. It got to the point where I would simply eat dinner and then about 15 minutes later, I would feel ill and throw up.

I went from 134 pounds to 117. Physically, I felt great. But it had its downside. One night I was asked over to an attractive man's house for dinner. He served lobster and a beautiful creamy dessert washed down with lots of wine. It was obvious he had plans for me after dinner, but by then I was throwing up so regularly that my body automatically went into action. I started to feel nauseated and I knew I had to get out of there. Fast. I arrived home just in time.

By now I was calling my little throwing up habit the "taste it twice diet." My friends did not think it was funny. One pal who joined me on a business trip and saw my after-dinner regurgitations was very upset. "You'll ruin your teeth and you could choke, you know." I curtailed my vomiting for the rest of the trip.

While my friends found it both disturbing and puzzling, I actually was happy with my successful dieting tools. They were effective and the euphoria I experienced while starving was addictive. But it all came to an end abruptly when I met my husband. It wasn't that he made me so happy that I quit. It was just that when I told him what I was doing, he became very upset and pleaded with me to stop. I did, but I was under constant surveillance. For years, if I ever got stomach flu or ate something that made me sick, he was right in there as I was throwing up, lecturing me about eating disorders.

When he moved out a couple of years ago, I wondered if I would go on my favorite diet again. I didn't. In fact, it wasn't until this spring, when I started dating a man 10 years my junior, that the starvation diet started up. Initially I was just trying to lose weight fast. The relationship was progressing at a greater speed than I had anticipated. So I was down to eating practically nothing and swimming a half mile every day.

All of a sudden, that wonderful euphoric feeling was back again. I felt terrific. I looked terrific. For three months I ate just enough to keep from fainting. Then I ended the relationship because it was becoming just a bit too much. I started eating again, but with restraint. And that's where I am now.

People in concentration camps who are starving feel euphoric, but apparently it's a transient feeling that goes away after a while.

But I'll starve myself again, for the sense of power over my body. It's almost an erotic feeling. I must admit that this summer, as I starved myself and fell in love again, I started to feel like Charlotte Rampling (feel, not look) as she wasted away in that isolated room with Dirk Bogarde in "The Night Porter." Feeling better about your body is extremely sensuous.

As I look back and read this, I notice that men seem to be involved in each one of these dieting episodes, although not in similar roles. Sometimes they are troubling, like that one during college. Sometimes they are absent and sometimes they are an exciting new beginning, as with the third. Not really any pattern.

But another thing I notice is that every bout has started off in the spring. Could the knowledge that a long Canadian winter is coming to an end be a catalyst for me to try to experience a rebirth as a new, thinner entity? Or is it just that as the parka comes off, my white, bumpy flesh is exposed to the world once again?

I think it's actually just circumstance. If I'm pushed into not eating for a day or two because of a nervous stomach, all of a sudden I find myself enjoying it. And so far, I've been able to control it, rather than have it control me.

I'll starve myself again, for the sense of power over my body.

If I'm this positive about it, would I want, say, my daughter to start starving herself? Definitely not. In fact, when she started to complain about her weight (which was perfect) a year ago, I told her all women feel fat—even the skinniest—so she shouldn't worry about it. And she stopped worrying. I don't want her to start because I'm concerned if she ever finds out how good it feels, she won't be able to quit. It is that kind of thing. If you can control it, it is a great dieting tool, but once it controls you, you're in real trouble.

I have friends who have starved themselves down to 80 pounds. I have known people who died because of their starving habit. So why do I play with it? I don't experiment with drugs that can kill me, so why do I dabble in such a dangerous dieting game? With anorexia and bulimia, I've always been on the precipice. As long as I can keep myself from tumbling off the edge, I have nothing to fear from it. And so far, I've been able to. So what's wrong with that?

Athletes Are More Vulnerable to Anorexia than Non-Athletes

Liz Applegate

Liz Applegate is a contributor to Runner's World *magazine.*

Athletes are believed to be more vulnerable to anorexia and other eating disorders than nonathletes. In particular, anorexia tends to strike most often among athletes competing in sports, such as gymnastics, running, and wrestling, that require lean body types. Researchers believe that because of the highly competitive nature of sports, equally competitive participants become obsessed with maximizing their performance. The character traits found in many anorexics, such as perfectionism and obsessive behavior, are usually traits that can be observed in highly competitive athletes. Experts think that competitive sports can trigger an eating disorder in an athlete with an obsessive and competitive personality.

Three female college students entered my office one afternoon desperate for advice that might help their roommate. "All Elise does is run," one of them told me. "She hardly eats anything, and she still thinks she needs to lose weight!" "We're just so worried about her," another said. "Elise is so skinny, but she denies anything is wrong. We want to confront her about it, but we don't know how." The third asked, "Do you think running started this whole thing?"

As you might guess, their description of Elise fit the classic profile of a person with the eating disorder anorexia nervosa. If left untreated, Elise's drive for thinness could land her in serious trouble, such as irreversible bone disease or even death. And these young women were right to be concerned that Elise's excessive running might be at the root of her eating and weight troubles. In fact, several studies have shown that compared with nonathletes, athletic men and women—especially those in sports in which body weight and shape are an issue, such as running, wrestling and gymnastics—have a greater incidence of abnormal eating behaviors and

Reprinted from Liz Applegate, "Running into Trouble," *Runner's World*, April 1, 1998. Reprinted with permission from the author.

the full-blown clinical eating disorders anorexia and bulimia.

So, for good reason, many runners question their own eating and exercise patterns. Many of us use running as a weight-control tool. And why not? Running burns calories, and it's good for you to boot. But sometimes we may find ourselves "running off" occasional indulgences—that is, using exercise to "make up" for our not-so-healthy eating habits. When this "eat-and-run" behavior becomes a compulsion, it may signal the onset of an eating disorder.

The quest for thinness

Though they occur mostly in young women, anorexia and bulimia can strike anyone. Anorexia consists of a cluster of behaviors and symptoms, including self-induced starvation, an intense fear of becoming fat, body weight that's 15 percent or more below the normal range for one's height, and, in women, amenorrhea (the loss of a regular menstrual cycle).

Despite their frail appearance, anorexics view themselves as fat. Their distorted body image drives them to lose more and more weight, primarily through severe calorie-cutting and excessive exercise, which gives them a feeling of control. Usually perfectionists and highly motivated people, anorexics are typically college educated, single and from middle- to upper-class families. But they have low self-esteem, believed to stem from an upbringing by overly protective or controlling parents.

Bulimia affects many more individuals than anorexia. By some reports, anywhere from 15 to 62 percent of all female college athletes suffer from this eating disorder. And, like anorexia, bulimia strikes most often among athletes in sports in which a lean physique is crucial to performance.

Bulimics indulge in frequent episodes of binge eating, during which they often feel a sense of helplessness and a lack of self-control. Afterward, their feelings of extreme guilt and self-disgust prompt purging of the unwanted calories (usually by vomiting or the use of laxatives and diuretics) to prevent weight gain. Some may use excessive exercise such as running or stair-climbing for hours as a means of purging. But because bulimics are usually normal in body weight and appearance, family and friends may be unaware of their battle with food.

Anorexia and bulimia don't develop overnight; many athletes may be suffering from what's called a subclinical eating disorder, a possible precursor to a clinical problem. According to leading researchers, athletes may take up abnormal eating behaviors such as skipping meals, 24-hour fasts, calorie restriction and occasional purging (maybe once a week instead of the two or more times per week seen in bulimia) as a means to lose weight. They may also be obsessed with their weight and very fearful of becoming fat. The number of athletes with a subclinical eating disorder is unknown, but the problem is believed to be rampant in such sports as gymnastics, crew, wrestling, volleyball and running.

Runners at risk?

With all this glum news about exercise and eating disorders, it's only fair to ask if running—or any exercise, for that matter—may trigger these abnormal habits. Some researchers theorize that commitment to an exercise program such as training for a marathon could lead to eating disorders for some personality types or may aggravate an existing problem. For example, psychological traits such as high achievement orientation and perfectionism are common both in people with eating disorders and in athletes. Such traits are usually essential for successful competition.

What this may mean is that, given the right conditions, some people with certain personality types may be predisposed to develop eating disorders. Dr. Jorunn Sundgot-Borgen of the Norwegian University of Sport and Physical Education in Oslo studies the factors that may trigger or exacerbate eating disorders in female athletes. In one study, she evaluated middle- and long-distance runners who were identified as "at risk" for eating disorders based on their scores on a specially designed questionnaire.

Dr. Sundgot-Borgen found that anorexia, bulimia and a subclinical eating disorder called anorexia athletica were likely to take hold when an athlete began dieting or experienced frequent weight fluctuations. Also, those athletes who started dieting at a younger age were more likely to develop a serious eating problem. A traumatic event such as an injury also appeared to set off eating disorders, perhaps because of forced inactivity, which in turn may have led to unwanted weight gain.

Psychological traits such as high achievement orientation and perfectionism are common both in people with eating disorders and in athletes.

Another potential trigger noted by Dr. Sundgot-Borgen was an abrupt increase in training volume that coincided with a sudden loss of weight, most likely due to the extra exertion. In any case, athletes weren't eating enough, and this lack of calories may have created a psychological and biological "climate" that prompted an eating disorder to develop.

Other researchers have noted that eating disorders in athletes may be connected to our genetic makeup. In fact, substance-abuse problems and clinical depression, both inheritable conditions, are common in bulimics and anorexics.

Triple trouble

Eating disorders bring with them a myriad of health problems. Low calorie intake or sporadic eating, for example, results in poor performance and endurance. When we cheat the body of food, our low intake of protein and key vitamins and minerals can weaken the immune system and lead to chronic illnesses and fatigue. Also, skimpy nutrition makes injuries more likely and slows recovery.

But more threatening to an athlete's long-term health is a condition known as the female athlete triad: an eating disorder in combination with amenorrhea and osteoporosis (the debilitating bone disease seen most often in elderly women). Researchers and health professionals have identified this serious complex of problems in many female athletes of all ability levels and ages.

While it's not clear which comes first, eating disorders and menstrual irregularities are connected. Many women athletes—including an estimated 25 to 40 percent of female endurance athletes—experience amenorrhea or missed periods. But among women with diagnosed eating disorders and even those with subclinical problems, amenorrhea is much more common. Though some women athletes may welcome this condition as "less hassle," the consequences are severe.

Depressed levels of the female hormone estrogen accompany amenorrhea, and with this deficiency comes bone-mineral loss, or premature osteoporosis. In fact, even in young women, calcium loss from the bones can cause stress fractures and even fractures of the vertebrae similar to those seen in 80-year-olds.

Treatment of the female athlete triad requires the help of physicians, dietitians and mental-health professionals. In extreme situations, especially in women with prolonged cases, hospitalization may be needed. And, as with other serious diseases, prevention is key. This requires vigilance on the part of parents, coaches and friends watching for signs of abnormal eating and exercise behaviors.

Like Elise's roommates, if you see a friend or loved one seemingly wasting away before your eyes, don't be afraid to get involved. Ask him or her to seek professional guidance and treatment and offer your help in finding that guidance. And if your friends and family are sounding the alarm by constantly saying you look gaunt and unhealthy, consider the possibility that they may be right. Talk to a counselor. Eating disorders are no trivial matter; they can be deadly.

Some Anorexics Should Have the Right to Refuse Treatment

Heather Draper

Heather Draper is an instructor at the University of Birmingham and a contributor to the Journal of Medical Ethics.

It is possible that some anorexics will never be cured and that forcing them to receive treatment will only prolong their lives rather than produce a permanent recovery. For these cases, it is important to make a distinction between decisions about receiving treatment and decisions about the quality of one's life. Although it may be perceived as irrational or involuntary for an anorexic to refuse food to the point of self-starvation, the same cannot be said about a chronic anorexic who refuses treatment because she feels the quality of her life is not worth enduring the torture of forced feeding. Perhaps in these chronic cases it is wrong not to allow the anorexic the right to refuse treatment.

Anorexia nervosa is classified as a mental disorder in the International Classification of Diseases (ICD-10), and between 20–30 anorexics die each year in the UK.[1] There is no consensus about what causes the disorder or how it is to be treated. Feeding without consent usually becomes an issue when without further nutrition the anorexic will begin an irreversible decline to death. Once their weight has stabilised and they are released into out-patient care, many will begin to starve themselves again. The natural cycle for the illness is anything from one to eight years. After eight years, the chances of cure begin to diminish rapidly, and it is also thought that ultimate success can also be adversely affected by repeated episodes of forced feeding.[2]

In August 1997, The Mental Health Commission issued guidance on when anorexics can be detained, treated and fed without consent.[3] Although these notes echoed the law as it already stood, the need for such clarification was highlighted in January 1996 by the death of Nikki

Reprinted from Heather Draper, "Treating Anorexics Without Consent: Some Reservations," *Journal of Medical Ethics*, February 1998. Reprinted with permission from BMJ Publishing Group.

Hughes. Acting on legal advice, her doctors refused to feed her without her consent, even though she was anorexic. The claim was that Nikki understood what she was doing and had the right to refuse therapy, even though it would result in her death. The Mental Health Commission guidance makes it clear that it would *not* have been illegal to feed Nikki without her consent, providing such feeding was part of a programme of therapy for her anorexia, or necessary to restore her to a condition where other therapies might have been effective.

Many anorexics feel constantly like alcoholics, that they are just one step away from disaster.

Although detention, therapy and feeding without consent may be justified in the majority of cases, one can still have reservations which concern a minority of anorexics whose needs cannot be overlooked simply because they are a minority. For instance, in October 1997, Samantha Kendall died after eighteen years of battling with anorexia. Her case made headline news because her twin sister had died three years earlier, also from anorexia. Her family were reported at the time as saying that Samantha wanted to die.[4] Can it be argued that in her case, feeding would simply have *prolonged* her life rather than *saved* it in the interests of a possible cure?

Also in 1997, another anorexic, Kerry, attempted to gain some control over treatment decisions by signing a living will in which she specifically stated that she did not want to be fed, or undergo other measures to prolong her life, if she became incompetent in the future. At the time she made her living will (with legal help) she was receiving therapy and felt optimistic about her recovery. Past experience, however, of being fed without consent (in her case, being literally held down and forced to swallow a high calorie drink) made her determined not to be fed without her consent again.[5] Is it possible that in some cases living with and receiving therapy for anorexia can become so burdensome that the prospect of death seems preferable? Were the terms of Kerry's living will reasonable?

The distinction between *prolonging* and *saving* an anorexic's life

In *Riverside Health NHS Trust v Fox*, the judge determined that feeding did constitute treatment for anorexia because other therapies would not be possible until there had been some steady weight gain. The claim that in some cases feeding may only be *prolonging* life, because an anorexic is incurable, is much more controversial.

O'Neill[6] attracted more criticism than support from psychiatrists[7] when he published a case study of an anorexic woman who was referred for palliative care. Offering palliative care to anorexics was considered to be collusion at best, giving up on them at worst.[8] This is an understandable response because many anorexics do recover, some after many years. Anorexia is not a terminal illness in the sense that death is inevitable even if treatment is given. With anorexia it is fair to say that where there is life there is at least the hope of improvement. It is nevertheless possible that some will never get well and that for such patients the misery of feeding and precarious, undesired weight gain will never result in the benefit of being able to look back with gratitude at the actions of carers, parents or partners who refused to give up hope. In such cases, it may be reasonable to draw a distinction between prolonging life and curing anorexia.

There is a difficulty, however, with identifying these cases. With other illnesses, it is accepted that a patient should be the lead partner in deciding when the hope of cure is outweighed by the burdens of the illness and the therapy. But because anorexia is categorised as a mental disorder—a characteristic of which is refusal to eat—and because years of starvation may affect an anorexic's competence to make her own treatment decisions, she is not allowed to call a halt to therapy. And neither are her carers, whose role it is not to give up hope either in the prospect of ultimate cure or in the abilities of the anorexic to find the cure within herself. It is an additional tragedy of anorexia nervosa that the tiny minority of incurable sufferers are trapped by the logic of the definition of the illness and the philosophy of the therapy.

Refusing therapy

In the UK, competent individuals have the right to give or refuse their consent to medical intervention. This right can be exercised with or without giving reasons, and irrespective of whether the reasons given are rational. This right also extends to the mentally ill, for the only interventions which can be given without consent are those administered in connection with their mental illness; other interventions are specifically excluded by the Mental Health Act. This was reinforced in common law in *Re C* when the court upheld the refusal of a schizophrenic patient, detained under the act, to have his gangrenous leg amputated. Professional carers are advised that the nature of the decision to be made and the nature of the information required to make it, are vital in determining competence.

Even though anorexia is a mental illness, it is not obvious that anorexics are incompetent to make *any* decisions for themselves. Some are being treated for anorexia whilst at the same time working in responsible jobs, running their own finances etc. They are likely to be totally incompetent only at the point of starvation. The view that anorexics are specifically not competent to make treatment decisions is based on the judgments that they are somehow driven by their anorexia (and their behaviour is, therefore, involuntary) and that they hold irrational views about their body image.

Perhaps in the context of making decisions about the quality of their lives it is wrong not to allow anorexics the right to refuse therapy.

My own—not uncontroversial—view is that it might be possible for anorexics to be incompetent to make treatment decisions but nevertheless competent to make decisions about the quality of their lives as anorexics undergoing therapy. Two different kinds of refusal of consent to therapy may be confused in the assessment of a small minority of anorexics. The first is the refusal to eat, which may be regarded as involuntary and irrational. The second is the decision to refuse all therapy (including food) because the quality of life with anorexia is not good enough to outweigh the burdens of the therapy. Any decision that life is not worth living can be challenged by someone else for whom life in similar circumstances does seem worth having. But whilst we are justified in questioning her decisions, are we right to exclude the anorexic from the decision-making?

Let us take a step back from the emotionally charged issue of anorexia and consider a parallel case—that of a woman who knows that with a radical mastectomy and chemotherapy she has a good chance of recovering from breast cancer but who refuses to have the surgery because, in her opinion, living with only one breast or no breasts at all will be intolerable. She is *also* making a decision based on her perception of her body image and we might think that this is an irrational perception. Nevertheless, operating without her consent is unthinkable.

Certain cases of anorexia permit a similar verdict. Anorexics who have suffered from the condition beyond the extreme end of the natural cycle are in a strong position to judge what life with anorexia is like and therefore are also in a position to determine whether prolonging treatment is worth the accompanying burdens. Crisp's experience of working with anorexics prompted him to write:

> (m)any anorexics feel constantly like alcoholics, that they are just one step away from disaster. When suicide occurs, it is often within this context. The individual is seeking relief from the endless terror and exhaustion of a battle to maintain her position.[9]

Perhaps in the context of making decisions about the quality of their lives it is wrong not to allow anorexics the right to refuse therapy. It will be difficult to determine which anorexics can competently judge that they have reached the end of the road so as to protect from themselves the majority who cannot. Equally, it will be difficult to watch them die when it is possible to prolong their lives. But these difficulties should not deter us from trying to do our best by all anorexics, not just the majority.

Notes

1. Crisp A. *Anorexia nervosa: let me be*. London: Baillere Tindell, 1990: 31.
2. Lewis P. Feeding anorexics who refuse food. *Food, glorious food*. Proceedings of a conference held at King's College, London, July 1997 (in press).
3. Mental Health Commission. *Guidance on the treatment of anorexia under the Mental Health Act 1983*. London: HMSO, 1997 Aug.
4. *Birmingham Evening Mail* 1997 Oct. 22: 1.
5. TV series: What's the story? Channel 5 1997 Nov 30.
6. O'Neill J. *American Journal of Hospice and Palliative Care* 1994;Nov:36.
7. Ramsey R.,Treasure J. Treating anorexia nervosa: psychiatrists have mixed views on use of terminal care. *British Medical Journal* 1996;312:182.
8. Russell J. Treating anorexia nervosa. *British Medical Journal* 1995;311:584.
9. See reference 1: 81.

10

Insurance Companies Need to Provide Coverage for Anorexia

Cynthia Fox

Cynthia Fox is a contributor to Life *magazine.*

Anorexia is a serious disease that kills more people than any other mental illness, yet insurance companies either offer minimal or no coverage for proper treatment. Some doctors spend hours each week arguing the necessity of their patient's cases with insurers that still deny coverage. While some eating disorder programs temporarily assume the financial burden for needy but uninsured patients, they cannot do so for long or will be faced with bankruptcy. As a result, many anorexics are either partially treated and released or do not receive care at all. Those who are partially treated generally end up worse than they were before. Anorexia, like any other life-threatening disease, needs to be sufficiently covered by insurance.

Crouching by a highway in 100[degree] Kansas heat, Jayme Porter shivers in a cold that doesn't exist. She's nauseated, but because she's starving, she's too weak to throw up; she's dizzy, but because there's no fat padding her bones, it's too painful for her to sit on the ground. Sundae-colored cows graze alongside oil derricks, and excess-crop fires simmer on the horizon. But Jayme perches at the edge of this world of plenty, looking as if she's barely there, for her body is cannibalizing itself.

An hour later, Jayme, 20, meets the Wichita hospital doctors she has traveled three hours from her home in Oklahoma to see. They make a surprising discovery. Since Wichita's eating disorders program reluctantly released her two months earlier—at a dangerous 40 pounds underweight—because her insurance policy wouldn't cover the stay, no one has been providing her medical care, even on an outpatient basis. She weighs 81 pounds. She has trouble finding a job; some employers think she has AIDS. She has a handicapped-parking permit (her ravaged heart makes it

Reprinted from Cynthia Fox, "Discovery: Starved Out . . . ," *Life*, December 1, 1997. Reprinted with permission from Time Life Syndication, a department of Time Inc.

difficult to walk), yet the parking space she uses most is at the gym where she works out obsessively. She's a severe anorexic, and the sister of a severe anorexic, yet because her insurance policy doesn't begin to meet her needs, she has been drifting from therapist to therapist, each assuming the others had been doing basic medical tests. None had.

Jayme is in for another surprise: Dr. Tamara Pryor, who has been treating her as an outpatient for one hour every two weeks, announces that even this may soon end. The Wichita program is about to go under for the second time in two years because so many patients lack adequate insurance. All studies indicate that the sicker Jayme gets, the more difficult it will be to cure her. Yet the sicker she's gotten, the less treatment she's received—and now she's faced with none. It's a situation her doctors understand, for in the past few years a bizarre paradox has emerged. Anorexia is the mental illness with the highest mortality rate—15 percent of the more than one million Americans who have it will die—yet it receives the least sufficient insurance reimbursement. But Jayme doesn't understand. "I'll still be able to see Dr. Pryor, right?" she asks. No one answers.

Managed care and anorexia

Managed care—the cost-cutting approach adopted by nearly all insurers—has gutted the eating disorders field in the past 10 years. In the mid-1980s severe anorexics would stay two to seven months in hospitals until they reached ideal body weight. But stays for severe cases now range from two days to two weeks, with some insurers imposing a $10,000 lifetime cap, enough to cover about 10 inpatient days, or, as in Jayme's case, a $30,000 lifetime limit. All this despite studies indicating that most patients released underweight need rehospitalization. Doctors now tell 70-pound patients they must be sicker before they can be helped, the equivalent of "sending patients with strep throat away, saying they can't be treated until it causes kidney failure," says Dr. Walter Kaye, head of the University of Pittsburgh's eating disorders program. Adds Stanford's Dr. Regina Casper: "We actually convert people into chronic patients."

Some doctors spend more than 10 hours a week arguing with insurers. "They wear you down with untrained reviewers, then make you go through three or four levels of appeals," says Dr. Arnold Andersen, who runs an eating disorders clinic at the University of Iowa. "It's like trying to stop the ocean." Insurers generally won't reveal their rejection criteria, never see patients and make all judgments by phone. As a result, Andersen says, "every third case that needs hospitalization is not allowed in now." Dr. Elke Eckert, head of the University of Minnesota program, says that 40 percent of her patients are discharged before they should be. Adds Dr. Dean Krahn, who headed programs at the University of Michigan and the University of Wisconsin that folded because of insurance problems: "Patients gain five pounds and are discharged now. You get their anxiety up as high as it can be because they've gained weight, but you haven't had time to do anything that will help them accept it. It's torture rather than treatment." The prediction of many doctors: The 15 percent death rate will rise.

In recent months the problem has become even more urgent, as doctors have realized there are only a few top-notch programs left. If you have a severe eating disorder now, you may find not only that insurance won't pay for your care, you may find, as Jayme Porter did, that you have nowhere to go.

Back home in Stillwater, the day after she discovered the Wichita program might close, Jayme eats an apple for breakfast instead of the juice, yogurt, meat, cereal, milk and two fruits prescribed. She heads for Oklahoma State University for the lab tests that should have been done months ago. Then she sets out on her daily walk wearing a 20-pound knapsack that "helps me work out."

The importance of adequate coverage

No one who spends a day with Jayme can wonder for long why severe anorexics need supervision. After her walk she returns to her trailer—the one her parents started out in and is now hers—parked outside the campus. She pours diet Mountain Dew into a 49-ounce tumbler, explaining it has more caffeine than other sodas and gives her a buzz. She slips on a neon-orange minidress ("I get a rush seeing my skeleton") and checks, as she does every day, to make sure her forearm fits in a circle formed by her thumb and finger. Then she spends an hour in a ritual typical of anorexics. She puts a cup of broccoli on a plate—the same plate every day—and places it on the couch under her arm, out of view. She slowly eats while watching *One Life to Live,* her favorite soap. She ponders yogurt and retrieves one from the freezer ("it's harder frozen, so you eat less"). By day's end she should have eaten 2,800 calories. But no one is watching over her, so she'll eat just 500.

Managed care—the cost-cutting approach adopted by nearly all insurers—has gutted the eating disorders field in the past 10 years.

The trailer is devoid of personal effects, save pictures of her family in heart-shaped frames. She points out a stuffed bunny left at her door by a college friend "who won't come in anymore because he can't stand to look at me." She notes that Prozac has helped her divorce herself from some elements of her past—for example, an obsessive neatness that kept her from allowing people to sit on her couch because "the cushions got squashed." But she still talks to her mother, an administrator at the university, four times a day.

Jayme says she used to go drinking every night with boyfriends until late last year, "when I lost the last forty pounds and scared them all away." Doesn't she want to date? "One of my main goals is to get married and have babies," she says brightly. But she hasn't had her period in 11 months, which causes her mother to say angrily, "I've come to accept the fact that I may never have grandchildren." Jayme has starved herself back into childhood—her skin is covered with lanugo, the hair infants are born with—and forward into old age. Her hair is thinning, her teeth are rotting, and the longer she goes without menstruating the more she risks bone decay. She is trapped between her future and her past.

Jayme and her 23-year-old sister, Julie, grew up in Agra, an Oklahoma town that once had high hopes. Agra expected to become the site of a large freight center, and in the 1920s, a town of banks, saloons, cotton gins and 1,000 residents sprouted in the middle of nowhere. But the freight center was located elsewhere, and by the 1970s, when Julie and Jayme were born into what had become the typical Agra home—a trailer—all that was left was a blind man's concession stand, three churches, a school with 10 children per grade, and a population of 336. The only nightlife could be found in tin-shack bars. It was the smallest of small towns, the last place some might expect to find eating disorders, which have been tagged "rich kids' diseases."

But studies indicate that bulimia is most common among the lower classes and that anorexia occurs all over the U.S. The drive to succeed can play a more crucial role in the disorders than class or location, doctors think. Certainly, the Porters had drive. The girls' father, Galen Porter, a construction supervisor who raised livestock and prided himself on "always having fun," even during his tour in Vietnam, served on the local and state school boards. When Agra made national news after a parent demanded that the novel *The Color Purple* be taken off school shelves, Galen voted against censorship. He and his wife, Kay, sheltered their children from the more prohibitive local customs—which included a town church's demands that women stay at home, marry young and never cut their hair—and encouraged them to succeed.

In the mid-1980s severe anorexics would stay two to seven months in hospitals until they reached ideal body weight.

Succeed Julie and Jayme did. Agra's school had no arts and few sports programs, but it did have 4-H, Future Farmers of America and Future Homemakers of America. Julie traveled the state with these organizations, winning speech contests while Jayme won sheep-showing contests. Both their bedrooms became shrines to achievement, their shelves stacked with trophies as tall as the pipes of a church organ. Both became one of only two in their grades to go to college.

Trouble hit when they were juniors in college. Their parents believe that for Julie, the discovery she wasn't going to be sorority president was the trigger: She lost 40 pounds in two months and landed in a hospital weighing 87 pounds. For Jayme, three years younger, her parents think it may have been the realization she hadn't excelled at anything since 4-H days. Both girls describe that period simply: "I had to be thinnest." As the last of their high school friends married, it was clear the sisters' ambition had spun out of control.

Julie was lucky. Although her mother's insurance policy picked up only $10,500 of the $73,000 bill for her nine-month stay at nearby Laureate Hospital, she was able to continue treatment because a bureaucratic error led Laureate to believe that welfare had taken up the slack. Even after the error was realized, Laureate let her stay on, swallowing more than $20,000.

Jayme was not so lucky. When she hit 90 pounds last January, Laureate refused to take her unless her parents paid the $35,000 balance on Julie's bill. Hearing of a program in Arizona called Remuda Ranch, Kay and Galen say they checked with a benefits coordinator who told them their insurance company, American Fidelity Assurance, would not provide more than $10,000. So they remortgaged their house to come up with an extra $23,000 to pay for 60 days. But Jayme would stay in Arizona only 35 days. Remuda told the Porters Jayme had to leave immediately because she was considered "noncompliant."

At home over the next few weeks, Jayme lost more weight. "There was no place else to go," says Kay. Then, suddenly, hope: Wichita's Dr. Pryor consented to treat Jayme first and fight the insurance company later. Pryor, who had been cured of anorexia at age 15, took one look at Jayme and checked her into the hospital's intensive care unit.

Jayme continued her downward spiral. Her weight dropped to 60 pounds, and she was in a state of hypothermia with a body temperature below 92[degrees]. Within days, Pryor, fearing Jayme would die, called the family to her bedside. "She couldn't lift the sheets over herself," Kay recalls. "If she sat up, her heart rate would go to 180, then would slow to thirty-two beats a minute, and when she tried to get out of bed, it went off the charts. The nurses said you could see the outlines of her organs through her skin. Galen or I would sleep with her every night. We were terrified that if we left her she would die." Julie says she couldn't look at her sister: "I thought I'd be sick. I've seen skinny, skinny girls but nothing like that. She said she wanted a Mr. Potato Head, so I brought her one, but she couldn't even stick the little pieces in him."

Jayme pulled through with feeding tubes and was admitted to the psychiatric ward. She began sessions with Pryor. But after three weeks hope fizzled again. "They couldn't afford us, and we couldn't afford them anymore," says Pryor. Having racked up a $50,000 bill in Wichita, none of which American Fidelity paid, Jayme was released on April 23 weighing 79 pounds.

Insurance company officials would not comment on the adequacy of their policy, but they did provide records showing that American Fidelity paid only $30,000 of the $180,000 in psychiatric bills hospitals charged them. Pryor, whose program has since closed, was upset she had to release Jayme. "We should be able to keep them in the hospital for weeks after they've achieved ideal body weight, so we can begin to control behavior," she says. "In 1994 the average inpatient stay of an anorexic here was twenty-one days—now it's two to four days. Patients are coming in so much sicker it's frightening. I've been notorious for forcing the hospital to swallow bills. That's no way to run a program. It's the craziest thing in the world."

Treating anorexia as any other mental illness

In May, a month after Jayme was released, the nation's top eating disorders specialists gathered at the annual convention of the American Psychiatric Association in San Diego. They had a new problem. The National Alliance for the Mentally Ill was lobbying for bills in 37 states that would require insurers to treat mental illnesses as seriously as physical illnesses. But NAMI hadn't recommended including eating disorders in any of the parity bills. So the doctors planned to take on both the insurance industry and their own profession. They would try to persuade NAMI to include eating disorders in its legislation.

"There's such bias," explained Illinois eating disorders expert Dr. Pat Santucci. "A congressman asked me, 'How am I supposed to convince a small-business man he has to pay for this girlie disease?'" NAMI postponed the meeting. About the bills, NAMI later explained, it can't risk combating the prejudices until the biology of these illnesses is better understood. Anorexia doctors can't afford many of their own patients, let alone their own lobbyists. They had to wait and watch as bills excluding eating disorders were passed in several states.

The results of poor insurance

It's summer, and Jayme sits in her trailer, eyeing the clock like an alcoholic before cocktail hour. When it's time for her workout, she says, "Yes!" and leaps out of her slouch with arms and legs akimbo, like a puppet jerked to life.

No matter how anorexia begins, many doctors believe that starvation and compulsive exercising become addictive, and this is clearly true for Jayme. At the OSU gym, she sits in a machine that's twice as big as she is, working out with weights as heavy as she is, for nearly two hours. "I'm so strong," she says proudly.

Sixty miles away, in her Tulsa home, Julie flops into a chair, looking as puppetlike as her sister. But resemblances to Jayme end there. Julie received six months of intensive treatment—group therapy, psychotherapy, nutrition and body image class, AA, career counseling, 24-hour monitoring—and it changed her life. She lost her rituals, lost her need to please the world. Her house is as cheerfully unkempt as Jayme's is spartan. She graduated from college in June and has developed a love she picked up at the hospital—art therapy. Now she's considering getting a master's.

Kay and Galen, $145,000 in debt, have seen strange times. They have lost faith in doctors, who keep telling them their daughters' health is a commodity they must purchase. "I'm scared stiff for any of us to get sick now," Kay says. Both shift from affection to disbelief when they speak of their girls, trying to recall which qualities which daughter has lost to her disease. The sisters say their parents can pretend their problems don't exist. And the family's dynamics have changed dramatically. Just when Julie and her parents should have been mending fences after her illness, Jayme began going through the same thing, distracting Kay and Galen's attention. Hurt, Julie rarely comes home. The lack of outside resources has made Jayme more dependent on her parents than ever, reflected in the sardonic tone she adopts when speaking to them. ("I'm just a manipulative little girl, aren't I, Mommy?" she says at one point, wrapping her arms around Kay's neck.) The girls, who have had to compete for attention and money, almost never speak to each other.

The Porters were once a family of go-getters who worked and played hard together. Now Kay and Galen sometimes act like kids wondering where the fun has gone. The sisters often act like parents exasperated with the children; the parents, who lie in bed every night wondering what they did wrong, have been rendered as emotionally and financially helpless as their girls. The Porters are as trapped in their love for one another as they are trapped in the clutches of a disease—and a flawed health care system—they don't understand.

Julie will likely survive, which becomes evident when she talks about her weight. "Ninety-eight pounds," she says, though she doesn't like to admit it "because it's still too thin." Jayme, too, is afraid to reveal her weight, 81 pounds, but for a different reason: "It's not thin enough."

11

Society Does Not Take Anorexia as Seriously as Other Diseases

Jennifer Braunschweiger

Many thin celebrities are targets of the media and are often labeled as anorexics. Talk show hosts deliver jokes about how all models must starve themselves in order to be successful. Our society has come to accept that skinny is synonymous with anorexia and, as a result, has trivialized a very serious and often deadly disease. By making light of such a terrible illness, we demonstrate our ignorance to the fact that living with anorexia is an agonizing experience. We must stop trivializing and mocking anorexia and begin to approach it with the same sensitivity and compassion that we do other serious diseases. Jennifer Braunschweiger is a freelance writer in New York.

The rumors were flying as fast as fiber optics could carry them: Calista Flockhart—a.k.a. Ally McBeal—was anorexic. Did you see her at the Emmys? So skinny! She must be sick. The speculation spread like a nasty virus, with articles on Flockhart's bony body cropping up everywhere from the *Star* to *Time*. The actress denied the rumors, but that didn't stop the snide stories—or the jokes. On *The Tonight Show,* Jay Leno presented the "McBeal TV Dinner," a meal of a few peas and a single lima bean. *TV Guide* featured a takeoff on an Altoids ad, depicting Flockhart holding a box of "ALLY-TOIDS" the "curiously thin" mints that are "guaranteed to make you sexy and popular."

At nearly five-feet-six-inches tall and a reported 102 pounds, Flockhart is certainly slim. But why did her weight loss inspire jokes and gossip, not concern? Would the rumors have been as mean-spirited if she'd been diagnosed with, say, breast cancer? Of course not. But anorexia has become a joke of a disease. We use the term to describe any woman who's skinny—whether she's perfectly healthy or possibly sick—and in doing so, we trivialize an illness that is excruciatingly real.

Consider these examples of "anorexia" misuse: In an April 2, 1998, *Chicago Tribune* article, a columnist remarked that "miniskirts look terrific

Reprinted from Jennifer Braunschweiger, "Stop the Anorexia Obsession," *Glamour*, February 1999. Reprinted with permission from the author.

on the very young, on the anorexic. . . ." In a July 9, 1998, *New York Times* article on a Spice Girls' CD-ROM, the writer described the market for good interactive music products as "anorexically thin." The disease's name is now simply a synonym for slim.

"Anorexic" is also used as a weapon in the ongoing woman-on-woman catfight. The genetically slender are asked by allegedly concerned female bystanders if they're—omigod!—anorexic? One *Glamour* reader says: "I was shopping, and a woman came up to me and asked if I'd always been 'like this.' Then she advised me to seek counseling for my supposed eating disorder. I've always been skinny, but she made me feel so bad I put down the clothes I'd wanted to try on, and left." Which makes us wonder: Since when is it OK to accuse people of having a disease?

And it *is* a disease. The National Institute of Mental Health (NIMH) says 1 percent of young women develop anorexia, and 2 to 3 percent develop bulimia. The woman who starves herself doesn't just get too skinny. As she misses meal after meal, she begins to suffer from depression, hair loss and poor circulation. In time, her muscles begin to waste away, and she has trouble breathing. She stops menstruating and, eventually, may develop low blood pressure and an irregular heartbeat, which can lead to cardiac arrest. An estimated 5 percent of college-age women exhibit anorexic or bulimic behavior. Not all seek treatment. However, of the women who do become anorexic, NIMH estimates that one in 10 will die from cardiac arrest, suicide or other medical complications. Women are starving themselves to death. But why?

Experts believe anorexia stems from a girl's need to exert control over a life that seems more and more chaotic as she copes with adolescence. "She may not be comfortable with the way her body is changing and all the feelings she starts to have as hormones begin flooding her system," says Paula Levine, Ph.D., director of the Anorexia and Bulimia Resource Center, in Coral Gables, Florida. "She may think, The one thing I can control in life is what goes in and out of my mouth." Girls who starve themselves may be experiencing fear of becoming sexually developed or, in some cases, self-hatred so strong that it makes them literally want to disappear. And yet, the popular idea is that they starve themselves simply because they are vain wanna-be models trying to squeeze into size 4 jeans—and so it's fine, even feminist, to mock such silliness.

That mocking devastates real anorexics. One Florida psychologist who counsels women with eating disorders says a client of hers once came in crying because she'd seen a morning news show featuring an interview with a group of models. As an on-set gag the models were given a single strawberry for breakfast. One strawberry, several women: The show made light of starving oneself, portraying it as a prerequisite for a model's success. "My patient felt as if the terrible disease she has is a joke to the rest of the world," says the therapist. "But an eating disorder is an agonizing illness—that fact really is minimized."

Calista Flockhart may or may not be sick. Either way, our reaction to her should be careful and compassionate, not cruel and catty. Let's not let the cries of anorexia's real victims get drowned out by one very loud meow.

12

Holy Anorexia and Anorexia Nervosa

Manisha Saraf

At the time that she wrote the following essay, Manisha Saraf was in the class of 1999 at George Washington University School of Medicine in Washington, D.C. This essay was an entry in the Alpha Omega Alpha 1998 Student Essay Competition.

Holy anorexia was a term used until the sixteenth or seventeenth century to describe the act of self-starvation in an attempt to reach a higher plane of spirituality and closeness to God. While there is no physical distinction between holy anorexia and modern-day anorexia nervosa, there has been a change in how society interprets, judges, and reacts to the behavior of self-starvation. Holy anorexia was respected by medieval society and considered to be a method a woman used to cleanse her spirit. There were no attempts to stop the behavior and it was not viewed as an illness. In contrast, modern society considers anorexia to be a mental illness that needs to prevented or treated and cured. Therefore, it is important to note that disease is not only defined by physical characteristics and behavior but also by evolving societal interpretations and perceptions.

The word *anorexia* is derived from the Greek terms *an* (lack of) and *orexis* (appetite). Despite these linguistic origins, the act of starvation has not only profound medical and cultural interpretations but also historical significance beyond the deprivation of food. This concept is illustrated through the examination of "holy anorexia" and "anorexia nervosa." The examination of these two entities reveals a commonality of certain symptoms despite an enormous difference in societal implication. This finding draws into question the definition of disease in a society and the forces that influence this meaning.

Holy anorexia is a term used up to the sixteenth or seventeenth century to describe a behavior of self-starvation in an attempt to achieve a greater spirituality and closeness to God. Holy anorexia was not consid-

Reprinted from Manisha Saraf, "Holy Anorexia and Anorexia Nervosa: Society and the Concept of Disease," *The Pharos*, vol. 61, no. 4, Fall 1998. Copyright © 1998 by Alpha Omega Alpha Honor Medical Society. Reprinted with permission from *The Pharos*.

ered a disease; it was, as Danish child psychologist Kal Tolstrup noted, "considered holy behavior, wholly admirable and an expression of piety."[1] It was seen as a respectable religious practice in medieval society. People with this condition denied themselves food, so as to cleanse their bodies of sin; desire for a thin body or preoccupation with weight was not a feature. The study of holy anorexia is impeded by the fact that there exist few case reports from this time. It is known, however, that this behavior was well respected by society, and several who exhibited holy anorexia eventually achieved sainthood.[2]

In contrast, *anorexia nervosa* is a modern term describing a psychological illness characterized by the principal symptom of self-starvation. It is relatively common in Western society.[3] In the American Psychiatric Association *Diagnostic and Statistical Manual of Mental Disorders*, 4th edition, it is characterized by: refusal to maintain body weight to 85 percent of that expected for age and height, intense fear of gaining weight, disturbance in perception of body weight or shape on self-evaluation, and amenorrhea in the postmenarche.[4] Other factors believed to be contributory include: over-involved mothers, poor self-identity, and a sense of ineffectiveness.[5] Strong emotional conflicts are known to have a role in this disease.

The study of holy anorexia is impeded by the fact that there exist few case reports from this time.

Although holy anorexia and anorexia nervosa appear related only by the common symptom of self-starvation, there are cases in which certain symptoms of these two entities overlap. In fact, several authors have examined whether they are variations of the same condition.[2,3,6] This paper will examine the case of St. Catherine of Siena, probably the most celebrated holy anorectic, and modern cases of anorexia nervosa with religious overtones. These cases highlight the role of societal and cultural interpretations in what constitutes disease. It is often thought that an illness is comprised solely of an objective set of signs and symptoms. These cases, however, illustrate that the concept of disease is much more complex and subjective, and can be profoundly influenced by nonphysiological factors.

The story of St. Catherine of Siena displays features of both holy anorexia and anorexia nervosa. Catherine Benincasa was born in the year 1348 as a twin, although her twin sister did not survive infancy. The twenty-third of twenty-five children, Catherine had a turbulent yet symbiotic relationship with her mother and struggled for an independent self-identity and autonomy.[7] At adolescence, she became preoccupied with the desire to avoid the prospect of marriage. It was at this time that Catherine restricted her food intake to bread, water, and raw vegetables. As years progressed, her food intake declined. Referring to her spiritual sustenance, Catherine said, "I have food to eat of which they [my family] . . . know nothing."[7] Her refusal to eat and her vomiting stemmed from a fear that food would contaminate her and rob her spirituality. Catherine also viewed food as being evil. She would vomit as a way to purge her body and soul of contamination; she saw food as a poison. Her confessor wrote:

> I asked her if she would allow a little sugar. . . . At once she replied: "Do you want to quench the little spark of life that still remains in this poor body? Anything sweet is poison to me."[7]

Toward the end of her life, Catherine refused all food other than the Eucharist. This meager nourishment was not sufficient to sustain her body, and she died, presumably as a result of cardiac complications of malnutrition. Tolstrup noted that, on this physiological level, there is not much difference between the death of St. Catherine and that of young modern sufferers of anorexia nervosa.[1]

Similarities of holy anorexia and anorexia nervosa

Unlike the case of a person with anorexia nervosa, Catherine's history does not include a desire for a thin body. In the medieval period, however, holiness was the virtue that was most respected in society.[8] Therefore, in one sense, religiousness in that society was probably analogous to thinness, which is considered the ideal for women in modern-day Western society. Despite her prayer and fasting, Catherine felt that she was never able to be fully pure and cleansed of her sins. In this manner, both the holy anorectic and the woman with anorexia nervosa obsessively strive towards ideals that they are never fully able to reach. Starvation is a common outward symbol of this struggle. When one purely looks at the facts of her case divorced from all cultural and religious influences of her time, one could see St. Catherine as having symptoms of anorexia nervosa.

Despite her prayer and fasting, Catherine felt that she was never able to be fully pure and cleansed of her sins.

There exist modern cases of anorexia nervosa that also have strong religious undertones. Anthropologist Caroline G. Banks worked with two anorectic women who perceived their self-starvation as moral and religious as opposed to an illness.[6,9] A woman named Jane with a history of abandonment developed anorexia nervosa in her early teens. She "believed her spirit to be heavy when her body was fat or overweight."[9] Fat was equated with sin. In a sense, this rationale is similar to that of St. Catherine, who believed that food was poisonous to her soul. In addition, many people in modern society believe that those who are overweight are somehow unable to resist temptation. This belief is not unlike the medieval thought that overconsumption of food was immoral. Another woman, named Margaret, said repeatedly that she lived only on "faith and prayer."[6] This idea of religion as being a form of pure and unadulterated nourishment is also reminiscent of the ideas of the holy anorectics. If these women had lived during the Middle Ages, their self-starvation probably would have been seen as a glorious and noble endeavor as opposed to an illness. Tolstrup has suggested that the modern form of self-denial and suffering may be an unconscious reaction to a "religious vacuum" created as a result of a decline in the church and rise of science upon medicine and popular thought.[1]

Whereas the death of young anorectics is considered a huge tragedy, the life and death of St. Catherine was viewed as glorious and spiritual.

Whereas the death of young anorectics is considered a huge tragedy, the life and death of St. Catherine was viewed as glorious and spiritual. In the medieval period, church and religion were so strong that they dominated most aspects of society. As disease always exists in a societal context, it was seen then in the context of religion. Internist Walter B. Frommeyer, Jr., wrote, "Disease itself was considered punishment for sins, and therapy consisted of prayer and penance."[10] Religion was medicine. In this time period, self-denial or asceticism was seen as a way of identifying with and experiencing the suffering of Christ, and hence a way to be cured of all ailments. This communal experience was seen as a holy bond and was respected by society. For medieval society, fasting and the Eucharist were perhaps the holiest traditions. Alan of Lille, a medieval author, wrote in his *Summa* for preachers, "Fast is medicine to soul and body. It preserves the body from disease, the soul from sin."[11] In the same manner that eating provides nourishment to the body, fasting was seen to feed the soul. In fact, overindulgence of food was seen to be sinful, whereas restraint was a revered quality. In medieval society, a woman subjecting herself to starvation to cleanse her sins and achieve greater holiness was respected, and her behavior was not discouraged. Instead of being seen as an illness, starvation was considered a virtue, as evidenced by the reverence of Catherine of Siena.

The cases of Catherine of Siena and the two modern-day anorectics seem similar, yet are drastically different. These women exhibited self-starvation citing religious themes, and displayed an obsessive attitude towards food and emotional conflict. All three kept their body weight low, had a fear of food or weight gain. Catherine, however, was made a saint, and her fasting was respected, whereas the two modern women were labeled as ill and treated by mental health professionals. These women, when analyzed purely on their behavior, in the absence of cultural context, appeared to be exhibiting the same symptoms. In the context of their respective societies, however, their starvation has very different meanings.

These cases illustrate the significance of society in the perception of that which comprises disease. Disease is more than merely the existence of certain symptoms; it is the interpretation of these symptoms in light of cultural beliefs and modern medical technology. Therefore, the definition of disease, particularly that which is psychological in origin, is far from static.

Defining illness

Several authors have attempted to define illness. German physician Michael H. Kottow developed a theoretical system of defining health and disease, in which he termed "core" illness as that which has held a constant classification as disease throughout time.[12] An example would be cholera. The other, "conditioned" diseases, are much more difficult to define and are constantly modified in response to socio-cultural variables and medical technology.[12] They are comprised of a group of symptoms that have not always historically been categorized as illness. The classification of a group of symptoms into the category of disease depends upon what the individual or society perceives to be a distress or an impairment in usual functioning. Within Kottow's framework, anorexia nervosa and holy anorexia fall into the category of "conditioned" disease. Holy anorexia in medieval society was not considered to be an impairment in functioning. In a society dominated by religion, this behavior was revered and respected. The purpose of every human being was to achieve religious salvation and purity, and the act of starvation served to further this goal. In contrast, anorectics in modern secular society are unable to perform daily tasks, such as working and caring for themselves, and therefore suffer an impairment in functioning. Thus, their behavior is culturally acknowledged as disease. Due to changes in the definition of disease, it would be as incorrect to conclude that St. Catherine was suffering from anorexia nervosa as it would be to say that Jane and Margaret were holy anorectics. History of science professor Charles E. Rosenberg expressed the view that a "disease is no absolute physical entity but a complete intellectual construction, an amalgam of biological state and social definition."[13]

In the study of medicine it is necessary to note that perception of disease is not static; it is constantly changing with social beliefs. Physicians are confident in their ability objectively to detect and diagnose disease. They, however, and all people, bring their own perceptions and cultural biases to what exactly constitutes illness. The starvation of Catherine of Siena was perceived as a respected form of self-sacrifice for a higher goal in medieval society. A similar type of behavior, in the cases of Jane and Margaret, however, is considered mental illness. These cases draw into question the concept of disease and how an illness can be defined by subjective societal variables as much as by objective physiological symptoms.

References

1. Tolstrup K. Incidence and causality of anorexia nervosa seen in a historical perspective. Acta Psychiatr Scand 1990; 82 (Suppl 361):1–6.

2. Bell RM. Recognition and treatment. In: Holy Anorexia. Chicago (Ill.): University of Chicago Press; 1985. pp. 1–53.

3. Brumberg JJ. "Fasting girls": Reflections on writing the history of anorexia nervosa. In: Smuts AB, Hagen JW, editors. History and Research in Child Development. pp. 93–104, Chicago (Ill.): University of Chicago Press. Monograph of the Society for Research in Child Development 1986; 50 (4–5).

4. American Psychiatric Association. Diagnostic and Statistical Manual of Mental Disorders, 4th ed. Washington, D.C.: American Psychiatric Association; 1994.

5. Hartman D. Anorexia nervosa—diagnosis, aetiology, and treatment. Postgrad Med J 1995; 71:712–16.

6. Banks CG. 'Culture' in culture-bound syndromes: The case of anorexia nervosa. Soc Sci Med 1992; 34:867–84.

7. Rampling D. Ascetic ideals and anorexia nervosa. J Psychiat Res 1996; 19 (2/3):89–94.

8. Bynum CW. Holy Feast and Holy Fast: The Religious Significance of Food to Medieval Women. Berkeley: University of California Press; 1987.

9. Banks CG. The imaginative use of religious symbols in subjective experiences of anorexia nervosa. Psychoanal Rev April 1997; 84(2): 227–35.

10. Frommeyer WB. Commentaries on the history of medicine. II. From the post-Hippocratic era through the eighteenth century. Ala J Med 1973; 10:465–77.

11. Alan of Lille. Summa, Chap 34. France, c. 1200. As quoted in Bynum, Holy Feast and Holy Fast, p. 44.

12. Kottow MH. A medical definition of disease. Med Hypotheses 1980; 6: 209–13.

13. Rosenberg CE. The Cholera Years. Chicago (Ill.): University of Chicago Press; 1962. As quoted in Brumberg JJ, "Fasting Girls", p. 98.

Organizations to Contact

The editors have compiled the following list of organizations concerned with the issues debated in this book. The descriptions are derived from materials provided by the organizations. All have publications or information available for interested readers. The list was compiled on the date of publication of the present volume; the information provided here may change. Be aware that many organizations take several weeks or longer to respond to inquiries, so allow as much time as possible.

American Anorexia/Bulimia Association (AA/BA)
165 W. 46th St., Suite 1108, New York, NY 10036
(212) 575-6200
website: www.aabainc.org/home.html

AA/BA is a nonprofit organization that works to prevent eating disorders by informing the public about their prevalence, early warning signs, and symptoms. AA/BA also provides information about effective treatments to sufferers and their families and friends.

American Psychiatric Association (APA)
1400 K St. NW, Washington, DC 20005
(202) 682-6000 • fax: (202) 682-6850
e-mail: apa@psych.org • website: www.psych.org

APA is an organization of psychiatrists dedicated to studying the nature, treatment, and prevention of mental disorders. It helps create mental health policies, distributes information about psychiatry, and promotes psychiatric research and education. APA publishes the monthly *American Journal of Psychiatry*.

American Psychological Association
750 First St. NE, Washington, DC 20002-4242
(202) 336-5500 • fax: (202) 336-5708
e-mail: public.affairs@apa.org • website: www.apa.org

This society of psychologists aims to "advance psychology as a science, as a profession, and as a means of promoting human welfare." It produces numerous publications, including the monthly journal *American Psychologist*, the monthly newspaper *APA Monitor*, and the quarterly *Journal of Abnormal Psychology*.

Anorexia Nervosa and Bulimia Association (ANAB)
767 Bayridge Dr., PO Box 20058, Kingston, ON K7P 1C0, Canada
website: www.ams.queensu.ca/anab/

ANAB is a nonprofit organization made up of health professionals, volunteers, and past and present victims of eating disorders and their families and friends. The organization advocates and coordinates support for individuals affected directly or indirectly by eating disorders. As part of its effort to offer a broad range of current information, opinion, and/or advice concerning eating disorders, body image, and related issues, ANAB produces the quarterly newsletter *Reflections*.

Anorexia Nervosa and Related Eating Disorders (ANRED)
PO Box 5102, Eugene, OR 97405
(503) 344-1144
website: www.anred.com

ANRED is a nonprofit organization that provides information about anorexia nervosa, bulimia nervosa, binge eating disorder, compulsive exercising, and other lesser-known food and weight disorders, including details about recovery and prevention. ANRED offers workshops, individual and professional training, as well as local community education. It also produces a monthly newsletter.

Eating Disorders Awareness and Prevention (EDAP)
603 Stewart St., Suite 803, Seattle, WA 98101
(206) 382-3587 • fax: (206) 829-8501
website: www.edap.org

EDAP is dedicated to promoting the awareness and prevention of eating disorders by encouraging positive self-esteem and size acceptance. It provides free and low-cost educational information on eating disorders and their prevention. EDAP also provides educational outreach programs and training for schools and universities and sponsors the Puppet Project for Schools and the annual National Eating Disorders Awareness Week. EDAP publishes a prevention curriculum for grades four through six as well as public prevention and awareness information packets, videos, guides, and other materials.

Harvard Eating Disorders Center (HEDC)
356 Boylston St., Boston, MA 02116
(617) 236-7766
website: www.hedc.org

HEDC is a national nonprofit organization dedicated to research and education. It works to expand knowledge about eating disorders and their detection, treatment, and prevention and promotes the healthy development of women, children, and everyone at risk. A primary goal for the organization is lobbying for health policy initiatives on behalf of individuals with eating disorders.

National Association of Anorexia and Associated Disorders (ANAD)
Box 7, Highland Park, IL 60035
(847) 831-3438 • fax: (847) 433-4632
e-mail: info@anad.org • website: www.anad.org

ANAD offers hot-line counseling, operates an international network of support groups for people with eating disorders and their families, and provides referrals to health care professionals who treat eating disorders. It produces a quarterly newsletter and information packets and organizes national conferences and local programs. All ANAD services are provided free of charge.

National Eating Disorder Information Centre (NEDIC)
CW 1-211, 200 Elizabeth St., Toronto, ON M5G 2C4, Canada
(416) 340-4156 • fax: (416) 340-4736
e-mail: nedic@uhn.on.ca • website: www.nedic.on.ca

NEDIC provides information and resources on eating disorders and weight pre-occupation, and it focuses on the sociocultural factors that influence female health-related behaviors. NEDIC promotes healthy lifestyles and encourages individuals to make informed choices based on accurate information. It publishes a newsletter and a guide for families and friends of eating-disorder sufferers and sponsors Eating Disorders Awareness Week in Canada.

National Eating Disorders Organization (NEDO)
6655 S. Yale Ave., Tulsa, OK 74136
(918) 481-4044 • fax: (918) 481-4076
website: www.kidsource.com/nedo/index.html

NEDO provides information, prevention, and treatment resources for all forms of eating disorders. It believes that eating disorders are multidimensional, developed and sustained by biological, social, psychological, and familial factors. It publishes information packets, a video, and a newsletter, and it holds a semiannual national conference.

Bibliography

Books

Suzanne Abraham and Derek Llewellyn-Jones — *Eating Disorders: The Facts.* Oxford, England: Oxford University Press, 1997.

Frances M. Berg — *Afraid to Eat: Children and Teens in Weight Crisis.* Ed. Kendra Rosencrans. Hettinger, ND: Healthy Weight Publishing Network, 1997.

Carolyn Costin — *Your Dieting Daughter: Is She Dying for Attention?* New York: Brunner/Mazel, 1997.

Lindsey Hall and Monika Ostroff — *Anorexia Nervosa: A Guide to Recovery.* Carlsbad, CA: Gurze Books, December 1998.

Marya Hornbacher — *Wasted: A Memoir of Anorexia and Bulimia.* New York: HarperFlamingo, January 1999.

Myra H. Immell, ed. — *Eating Disorders.* San Diego: Greenhaven Press, 1999.

Bryan Lask and Rachel Bryant-Waugh, eds. — *Anorexia Nervosa and Related Eating Disorders in Childhood and Adolescence.* Philadelphia, PA: Psychology Press, September 1999.

Steven Levenkron — *Treating and Overcoming Anorexia Nervosa.* New York: Warner Books, 1997.

Judy Sargent — *The Long Road Back: A Survivor's Guide to Anorexia.* Georgetown, MA: North Star, 1999.

Periodicals

Donald Demarco — "Anorexia and the Misinformation Explosion," *Culture Wars*, September 1997.

Nancy K. Dess — "Killer Workout: The Dark Side of Diet and Exercise," *Psychology Today*, May/June 2000.

Denise Grady — "Efforts to Fight Eating Disorders May Backfire," *New York Times*, May 7, 1997.

Katherine A. Halmi — "A 24-Year-Old Woman with Anorexia Nervosa," *JAMA*, June 24, 1998.

Patricia Hittner — "Dying to Be Thin," *Better Homes and Gardens*, August 1997.

Caroline Knapp — "Body Language: Are People with Eating Disorders Desperate for Control or Just Too Sensitive for Their Own Good?" *New York Times Book Review*, January 4, 1998.

Carol Krucoff — "Is Your Child Dying to Win?" *Washington Post*, March 3, 1998. Available from 1150 15th St. NW, Washington, DC 20071.

Linda Davis Kyle   "Super Heroes and Super Models," *Professional Counselor*, December 1999.

Marty McCormack   "The Fight with Food," *Focus on the Family*, April 2000.

Mark Munro   "Loving an Anorexic," *Mademoiselle*, October 1997.

Susan Okie   "Anorexia May Depend in Part on Genes," *Washington Post*, January 27, 1998.

Leslie Vreeland   "Dying to Be Thin—After 30," *Good Housekeeping*, March 1998.

Pippa Wysong   "Anorexia Nervosa Patients Can Expect to Live a Normal Life Again," *Medical Post,* July 20, 1999.

Index